Congressional Research Service

Poverty in the United States: 2012

Thomas Gabe
Specialist in Social Policy

November 13, 2013

Congressional Research Service
7-5700
www.crs.gov
RL33069

CRS Report for Congress
Prepared for Members and Committees of Congress

Summary

In 2012, 46.5 million people were counted as poor in the United States—the number, statistically unchanged over the past three years, is the largest recorded in the measure's 54-year history. The *poverty rate*, or percent of the population considered poor under the official definition, was reported at 15.0% in 2012, a level statistically unchanged from the two previous years. The 2012 poverty rate of 15.0% is well above its most recent pre-recession low of 12.3% (2006) and remains at a level not last seen since 1993. Poverty in the United States increased markedly from 2007 through 2010, in tandem with the economic recession (officially marked as running from December 2007 to June 2009). Little if any improvement in the level of "official" U.S. poverty has been seen since the recession's official end, with the poverty rate remaining at about 15% for the past three years. Some analysts expect U.S. poverty to remain above pre-recession levels through much, if not most, of the remainder of the decade, given the slow pace of economic recovery. The pre-recession poverty rate of 12.3% in 2006 was well above the 2000 rate of 11.3%, which marked an historical low (a rate statistically tied with the previous historical low of 11.1% in 1973).

The incidence of poverty varies widely across the population according to age, education, labor force attachment, family living arrangements, and area of residence, among other factors. Under the official poverty definition, an average family of four was considered poor in 2012 if its pre-tax cash income for the year was below $23,492.

The measure of poverty currently in use was developed some 50 years ago, and was adopted as the "official" U.S. statistical measure of poverty in 1969. Except for minor technical changes, and adjustments for price changes in the economy, the "poverty line" (i.e., the income thresholds by which families or individuals with incomes that fall below are deemed to be poor) is the same as that developed nearly a half century ago, reflecting a notion of economic need based on living standards that prevailed in the mid-1950s.

Moreover, poverty as it is currently measured only counts families' and individuals' pre-tax money income against the poverty line in determining whether or not they are poor. In-kind benefits, such as benefits under the Supplemental Nutrition Assistance Program (SNAP, formerly named the Food Stamp program) and housing assistance are not accounted for under the "official" poverty definition, nor are the effects of taxes or tax credits, such as the Earned Income Tax Credit (EITC) or Child Tax Credit (CTC). In this sense, the "official" measure fails to capture the effects of a variety of programs and policies specifically designed to address income poverty.

A congressionally commissioned study conducted by a National Academy of Sciences (NAS) panel of experts recommended, some 19 years ago, that a new U.S. poverty measure be developed, offering a number of specific recommendations. The Census Bureau, in partnership with the Bureau of Labor Statistics (BLS), has developed a Supplemental Poverty Measure (SPM) designed to implement many of the NAS panel recommendations. The SPM is to be considered a "research" measure, to supplement the "official" poverty measure. Guided by new research, the Census Bureau and BLS intend to improve the SPM over time. The "official" statistical poverty measure will continue to be used by programs that use it as the basis for allocating funds under formula and matching grant programs. The Department of Health and

Human Services (HHS) will continue to issue poverty income guidelines derived from "official" Census Bureau poverty thresholds. HHS poverty guidelines are used in determining individual and family income eligibility under a number of federal and state programs. Estimates from the SPM differ from the "official" poverty measure and are presented in a final section of this report.

Contents

Figures

Tables

Appendixes

Contacts

Trends in Poverty[1]

In 2012, the U.S. poverty rate was 15.0%—46.5 million persons were estimated as having income below the official poverty line. Neither the poverty rate nor the number of persons counted as poor in 2012 differed statistically from 2011 or 2010. In 2012, an estimated 10.0 million more people were poor than in 2006 and the poverty rate (15.0%) was 22% above that of 2006 (12.3%). The 46.5 million persons counted as poor in 2012 is the largest number counted in the measure's recorded history, which goes back as far as 1959, and the 2012 poverty rate of 15.0% is the highest seen since 1993. (See **Figure 1**.)

The increase in poverty since 2006 reflects the effects of the economic recession that began in December 2007.[2] The level of poverty tends to follow the economic cycle quite closely, tending to rise when the economy is faltering and fall when the economy is in sustained growth. This most recent recession, which officially ended in June 2009, was the longest recorded (18 months) in the post-World War II period. Even as the economy recovers, poverty is expected to remain high, as poverty rates generally do not begin to fall until economic expansion is well underway. Given the depth and duration of the recession, and the projected slow recovery, it will likely take several years or more before poverty rates recede to their 2006 pre-recession level.

The poverty rate increased markedly over the past decade, in part a response to two economic recessions. A strong economy during most of the 1990s is generally credited with the declines in poverty that occurred over the latter half of that decade, resulting in a record-tying, historical low poverty rate of 11.3% in 2000 (a rate statistically tied with the previous lowest recorded rate of 11.1% in 1973). The poverty rate increased each year from 2001 through 2004, a trend generally attributed to economic recession (March 2001 to November 2001), and failed to recede appreciably before the onset of the December 2007 recession. Over the course of the most recent recession, the unemployment rate increased from 4.9% (January 2008) to 7.2% (December 2008), and continued to rise over most of 2009, peaking at 10.1% in October. From December 2009 to December 2010, the unemployment rate fell 0.5%, from 9.9% to 9.4%, but the poverty rate in 2010 increased over 2009. The unemployment rate fell 0.9%, from 9.4% to 8.5% from December 2010 to December 2011, and by December 2012 by an additional 0.7%, to 7.8%, but the poverty rate in 2012 (15.0%) has remained at recent peak levels for three years running.

The recession especially affected non-aged adults (persons age 18 to 64) and children. (See **Figure 2**.) The poverty rate of non-aged adults reached 13.8% in 2010, the highest it has been since the early 1960s.[3] In 2012 and 2011, the non-aged poverty rate of 13.7% was statistically no different than in 2010. The poverty rate for non-aged adults will need to fall to 10.8% to reach its 2006 pre-recession level.

In 2012, over one in five children (21.3%) were poor, a rate statistically unchanged from the two prior years, but significantly above its 2006 pre-recession low, at which time about one in six

---

[1] Supporting data are based on the following: U.S. Census Bureau, Income, Poverty, and Health Insurance Coverage in the United States: 2012; Current Population Report No. P60-245, September 2013; and unpublished Census Bureau tables, available on the Internet at http://www.census.gov/hhes/www/poverty/data/incpovhlth/2012/index html.

[2] Periods of recession are officially defined by the National Bureau of Economic Research (NBER) Business Cycle Dating Committee. See http://www nber.org/cycles/main html.

[3] The poverty rate of non-aged adults was 17.0% in 1959. Comparable estimates are not available from 1960 through 1965. By 1966, the non-aged poverty rate stood at 10.5%. See **Table A-1**.

children (16.9%) were counted as poor. Child poverty appears to be especially sensitive to economic cycles, as it often takes two working parents to support a family, and a loss of work by one may put the family at risk of falling into poverty.[4] Moreover, one-third of all children in the country live with only one parent, making them even more prone to falling into poverty when the economy falters.

In 2012, the aged poverty rate (9.1%) was statistically tied with most recent prior years, and in spite of the recession, remains at an historic low level. The longer-term secular trend in poverty has been affected by changes in household and family composition and by government income security and transfer programs. In 1959, over one-third (35.2%) of persons age 65 and over were poor, a rate well above that of children (26.9%). Social Security, in combination with a maturing pension system, has helped greatly to reduce the incidence of poverty among the aged over the years, and as recent evidence seems to show, it has helped protect them during the economic downturn.

The U.S. "Official" Definition of Poverty[5]

The Census Bureau's poverty thresholds form the basis for statistical estimates of poverty in the United States.[6] The thresholds reflect crude estimates of the amount of money individuals or families, of various size and composition, need per year to purchase a basket of goods and services deemed as "minimally adequate," according to the living standards of the early 1960s. The thresholds are updated each year for changes in consumer prices. In 2012, for example, the average poverty threshold for an individual living alone was $11,720; for a two-person family, $14,937; and for a family of four, $23,492.[7]

The current official U.S. poverty measure was developed in the early 1960s using data available at the time. It was based on the concept of a minimal standard of food consumption, derived from research that used data from the U.S. Department of Agriculture's (USDA's) 1955 Food Consumption Survey. That research showed that the average U.S. family spent one-third of its pre-tax income on food. A standard of food adequacy was set by pricing out the USDA's Economy Food Plan—a bare-bones plan designed to provide a healthy diet for a temporary period when funds are low. An overall poverty income level was then set by multiplying the food plan by three, to correspond to the findings from the 1955 USDA Survey that an average family spent one-third of its pre-tax income on food and two-thirds on everything else.

The "official" U.S. poverty measure[8] has changed little since it was originally adopted in 1969, with the exception of annual adjustments for overall price changes in the economy, as measured

[4] CRS Report RL33615, *Parents' Work and Family Economic Well-Being*, by Thomas Gabe and Gene Falk.

[5] For a more complete discussion of the U.S. poverty measure, see CRS Report R41187, *Poverty Measurement in the United States: History, Current Practice, and Proposed Changes*, by Thomas Gabe.

[6] The Department of Health and Human Services (HHS) releases poverty income guidelines that are derived directly from Census poverty thresholds. These guidelines, a simplified approximation of the Census poverty thresholds, are used by HHS and other federal agencies for administering programs, particularly for determining program eligibility. For current guidelines and methods for their computation, see http://aspe hhs.gov/poverty/index.shtml.

[7] See http://www.census.gov/hhes/www/poverty/data/threshld/index.html.

[8] The poverty measure was adopted as the "official poverty measure" by a directive issued in 1969 by the Bureau of the Budget, now the Office of Management and Budget (OMB). The directive was revised in 1978 to include revisions to poverty thresholds and procedures for updating thresholds for inflation using the Consumer Price Index (CPI). See OMB (continued...)

by the Consumer Price Index for all Urban Consumers (CPI-U). Thus, the poverty line reflects a measure of economic need based on living standards that prevailed in the mid-1950s. It is often characterized as an "absolute" poverty measure, in that it is not adjusted to reflect changes in needs associated with improved standards of living that have occurred over the decades since the measure was first developed. If the same basic methodology developed in the early 1960s was applied today, the poverty thresholds would be over three times higher than the current thresholds.[9]

Persons are considered poor, for statistical purposes, if their family's countable money income is below its corresponding poverty threshold. Annual poverty estimates are based on a Census Bureau household survey (Annual Social and Economic Supplement to the Current Population Survey, CPS/ASEC, conducted February through April). The official definition of poverty counts most sources of money income received by families during the prior year (e.g., earnings, social security, pensions, cash public assistance, interest and dividends, alimony, and child support, among others). For purposes of officially counting the poor, noncash benefits (such as the value of Medicare and Medicaid, public housing, or employer provided health care) and "near cash" benefits (e.g., food stamps, renamed Supplemental Assistance Nutrition (SNAP) benefits beginning in FY2009) are not counted as income, nor are tax payments subtracted from income, nor are tax credits added (e.g., Earned Income Tax Credit (EITC)). Many believe that these and other benefits should be included in a poverty measure so as to better reflect the effects of government programs on poverty.

The Census Bureau, in partnership with the Bureau of Labor Statistics (BLS), has recently released a Supplemental Poverty Measure (SPM), designed to address many of the perceived flaws of the "official" measure. The SPM is discussed in a separate section at the end this report (see "The Research Supplemental Poverty Measure").

(...continued)

Statistical Policy Directive 14, available on the Internet at http://www.census.gov/hhes/povmeas/methodology/ombdir14 html.

[9] Based on U.S. Department of Labor Bureau of Labor Statistics Consumer Expenditure Survey data, in 2012 the average family spent an estimated 10.0% of pre-tax income on food (including food consumed at home and away from home), as opposed to one-third in the mid-1950s. This implies that the multiplier for updating poverty thresholds based on food consumption would be 10.0 (i.e., 1/0.10), or 3.3 times the multiplier of 3 subsumed under poverty thresholds developed in the 1960s. Author's calculations from: http://bls.gov/cex/2012/aggregate/age.pdf.

Figure 1. Trend in Poverty Rate and Number of Poor Persons: 1959-2012, and Unemployment Rate from January 1959 through August 2013

(recessionary periods marked in red)

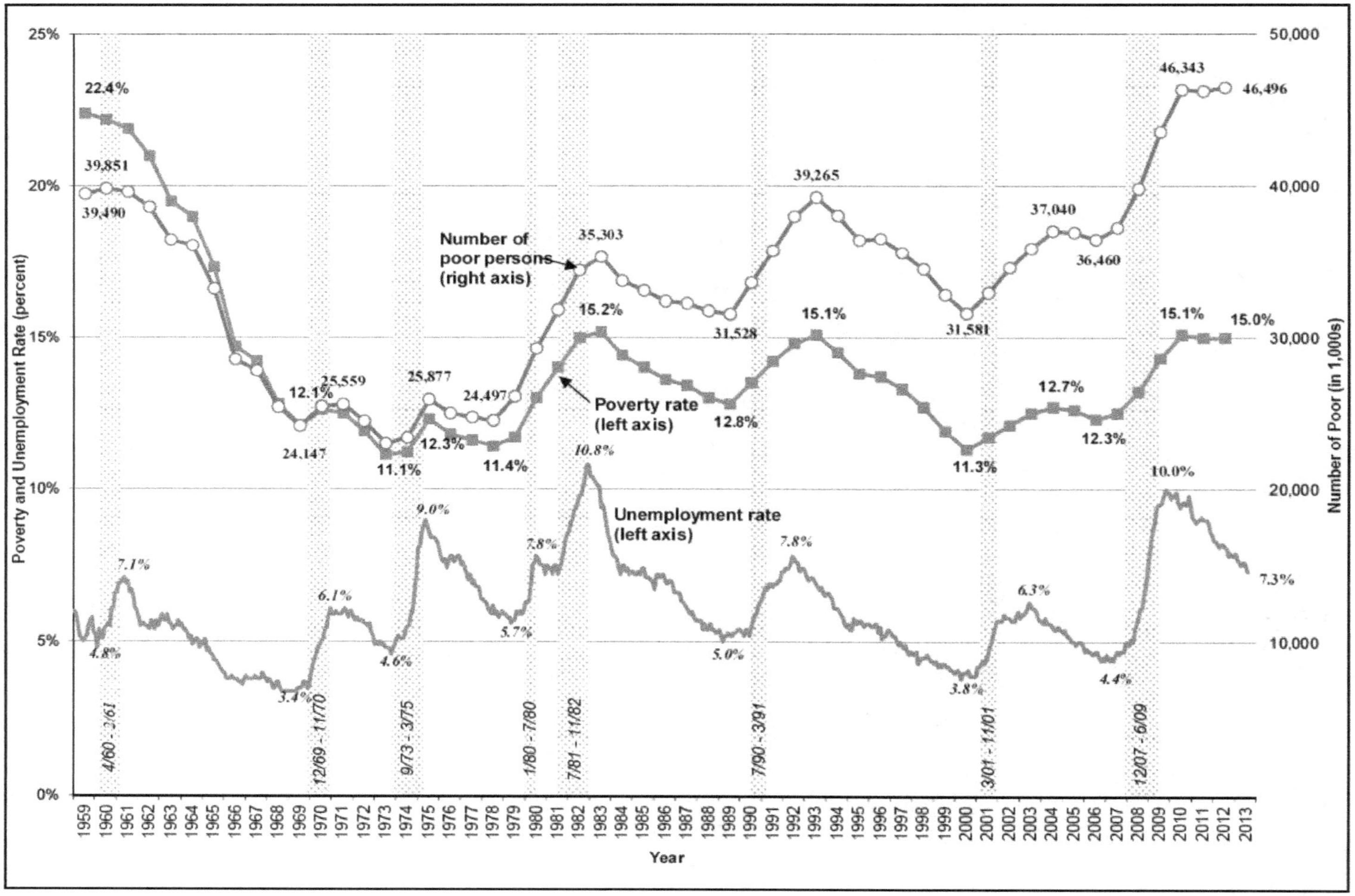

Source: Prepared by the Congressional Research Service (CRS) using U.S. Census Bureau, "Income, Poverty, and Health Insurance Coverage in the United States: 2012," Table B-1, Current Population Report P60-245, September 2013 available on the Internet at http://www.census.gov/prod/2013pubs/p60-245.pdf. Unemployment rates are available on the Internet at http://www.bls.gov/cps/. Recessionary periods defined by National Bureau of Economic Research Business Cycle Dating Committee: http://www.nber.org/cycles/main.html.

Figure 2. U.S. Poverty Rates by Age Group, 1959-2012

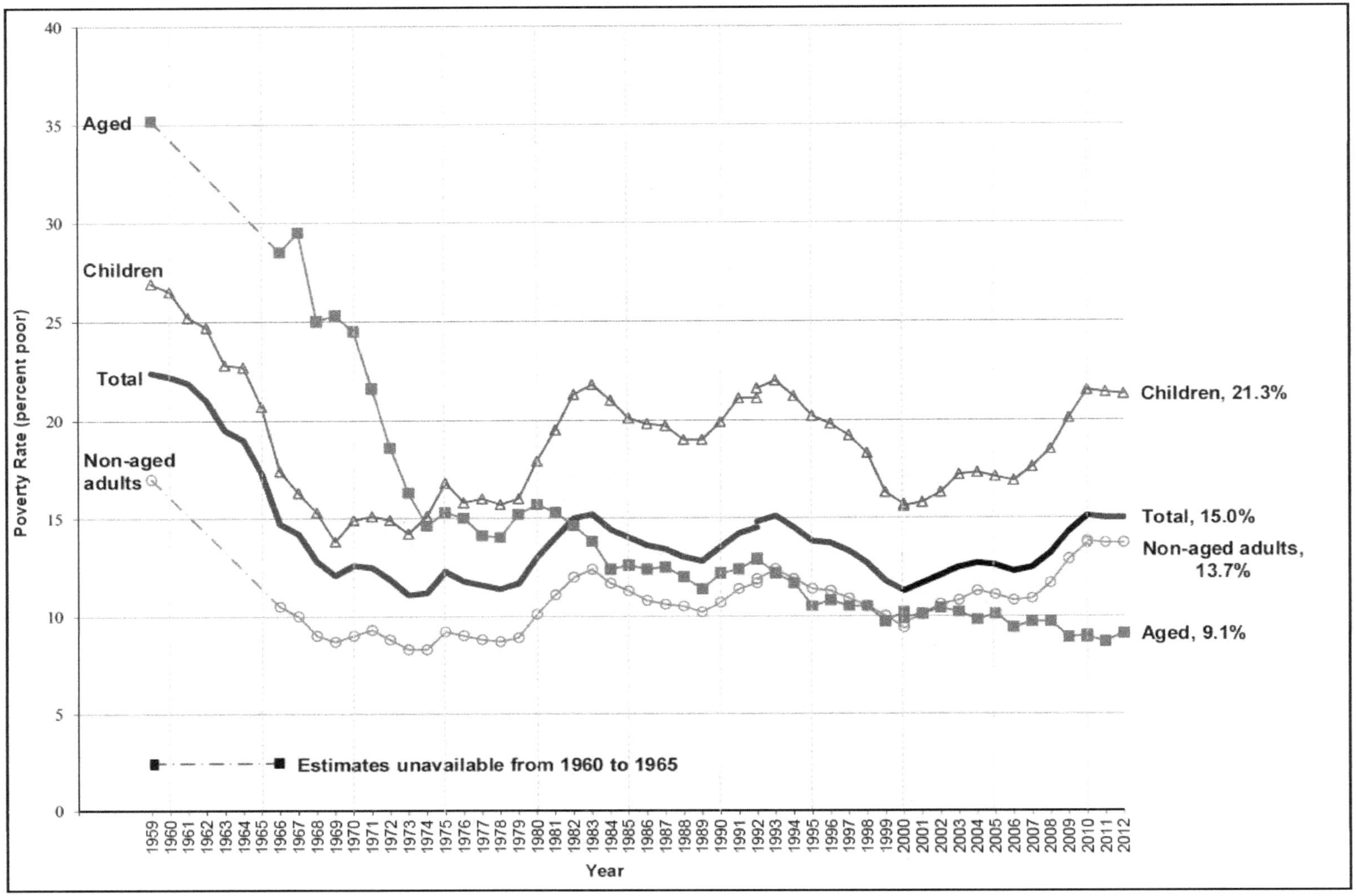

Source: Prepared by the Congressional Research Service using U.S. Census Bureau, "Income, Poverty, and Health Insurance Coverage in the United States: 2012," Tables B-1 and B-2, Current Population Report P60-245, September 2013, available on the Internet at http://www.census.gov/prod/2013pubs/p60-245.pdf.

Poverty among Selected Groups

Even during periods of general prosperity, poverty is concentrated among certain groups and in certain areas. Minorities; women and children; the very old; the unemployed; and those with low levels of educational attainment, low skills, or disability, among others, are especially prone to poverty.

Racial and Ethnic Minorities[10]

The incidence of poverty among African Americans and Hispanics exceeds that of whites by several times. In 2012, 27.2% of blacks (10.9 million) and 25.6% of Hispanics (13.6 million) had incomes below poverty, compared to 9.7% of non-Hispanic whites (18.9 million) and 11.7% of Asians (1.9 million). Although blacks represent only 12.9% of the total population, they make up 23.5% of the poor population; Hispanics, who represent 17.1% of the population, account for 29.3% of the poor. Poverty rates for all groups mentioned above were statistically unchanged from 2011 to 2012, as were the total numbers estimated as poor.

Nativity and Citizenship Status

In 2012, among the native-born population, 14.3% (38.8 million) were poor. Among the foreign-born population, 19.7% (7.7 million) were poor in 2012. The poverty rate among foreign-born naturalized citizens (12.4%, in 2012) was lower than that of the native-born U.S. population. In 2012, the poverty rate of non-citizens (24.9%) was about 10 percentage points above that of the native-born population (14.3%). In that year, the 5.4 million non-citizens who were counted as poor accounted for about one in nine of all poor persons (46.5 million). Poverty rates and the number estimated as poor, for each nativity/citizenship status highlighted above, were statistically unchanged from 2011 to 2012.

Children

In 2012, over one in five children (21.3%) in the United States, some 15.4 million, were poor—both their poverty rate and estimated number poor were statistically unchanged from 2011. The lowest recorded rate of child poverty was in 1969, when 13.8% of children were counted as poor.

Children living in single female-headed families are especially prone to poverty. In 2012 a child living in a single female-headed family was well over four times more likely to be poor than a child living in a married-couple family. In 2012, among all children living in single female-headed families, 47.2% were poor. In contrast, among children living in married-couple families, 11.1% were poor. The increased share of children who live in single female-headed families has contributed to the high overall child poverty rate. In 2012, one quarter (25.3%) of children were

[10] Beginning with the March 2003 CPS, the Census Bureau allows survey respondents to identify themselves as belonging to one or more racial groups. In prior years, respondents could select only one racial category. Consequently, poverty statistics for different racial groups for 2002 and after are not directly comparable to earlier years' data. The terms black and white, above, refer to persons who identified with only a single racial group. The term Hispanic refers to individuals' ethnic, as opposed to racial, identification. Hispanics may be of any race.

living in single female-headed families, more than double the share who lived in such families when the *overall* child poverty rate was at a historical low (1969). Among all poor children, well over half (56.1%) were living in single female-headed families in 2012.

In 2012, 37.5% of black children were poor (4.1 million), compared to 33.3% of Hispanic children (5.7 million) and 11.8% of non-Hispanic white children (4.4 million). (See **Figure 3**.) Among children living in single female-headed families, more than half of black children (53.3%) and Hispanic children (54.7%) were poor; in contrast, over one-third of non-Hispanic white children (36.5%) were poor. The poverty rate among Hispanic children who live in married-couple families (23.6%) was about half-again as high as that of black children (15.0%), and nearly four times that of non-Hispanic white children (6.2%) who live in such families. Contributing to the high rate of overall black child poverty is the large share of black children who live in single female-headed families (54.3%) compared to Hispanic children (29.6%) or non-Hispanic white children (16.1%). (See **Figure 4**.)

Figure 3. Child Poverty Rates by Family Living Arrangement, Race and Hispanic Origin, 2012

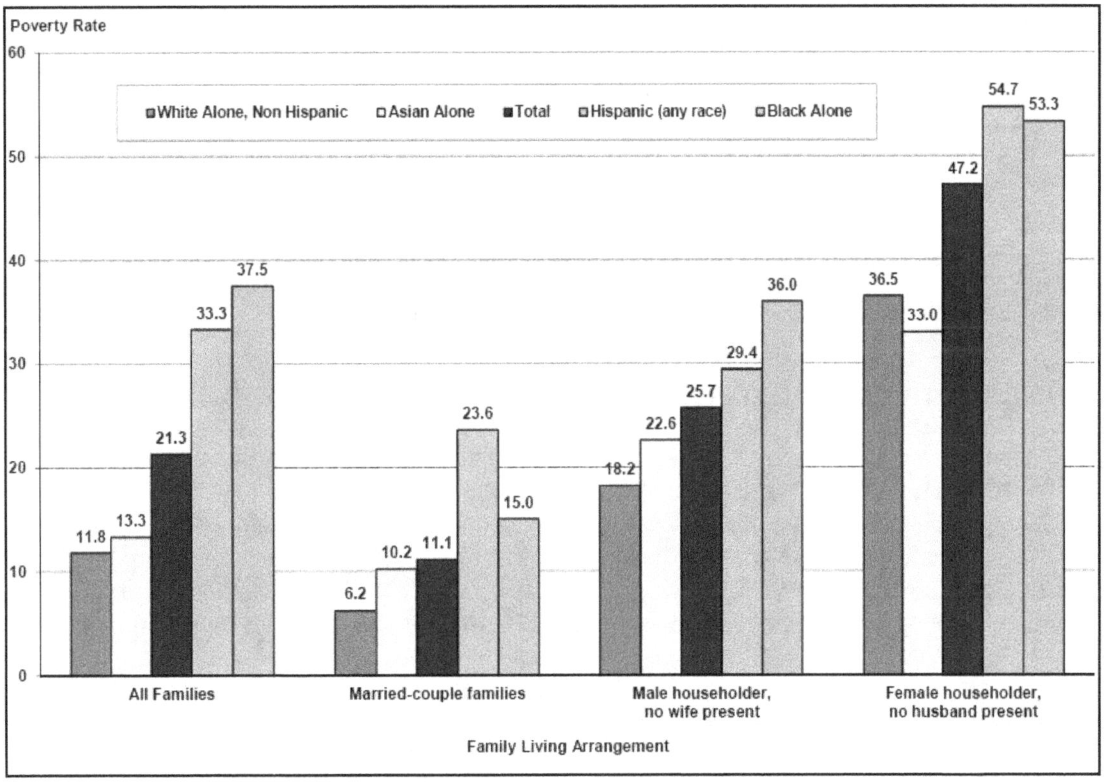

Source: Figure prepared by the Congressional Research Service (CRS) based on U.S. Census Bureau data from the 2013 Current Population Survey Annual Social and Economic Supplement, available at http://www.census.gov/hhes/www/cpstables/032013/pov/pov05_000.htm.

Figure 4. Composition of Children, by Family Type, Race and Hispanic Origin, 2012

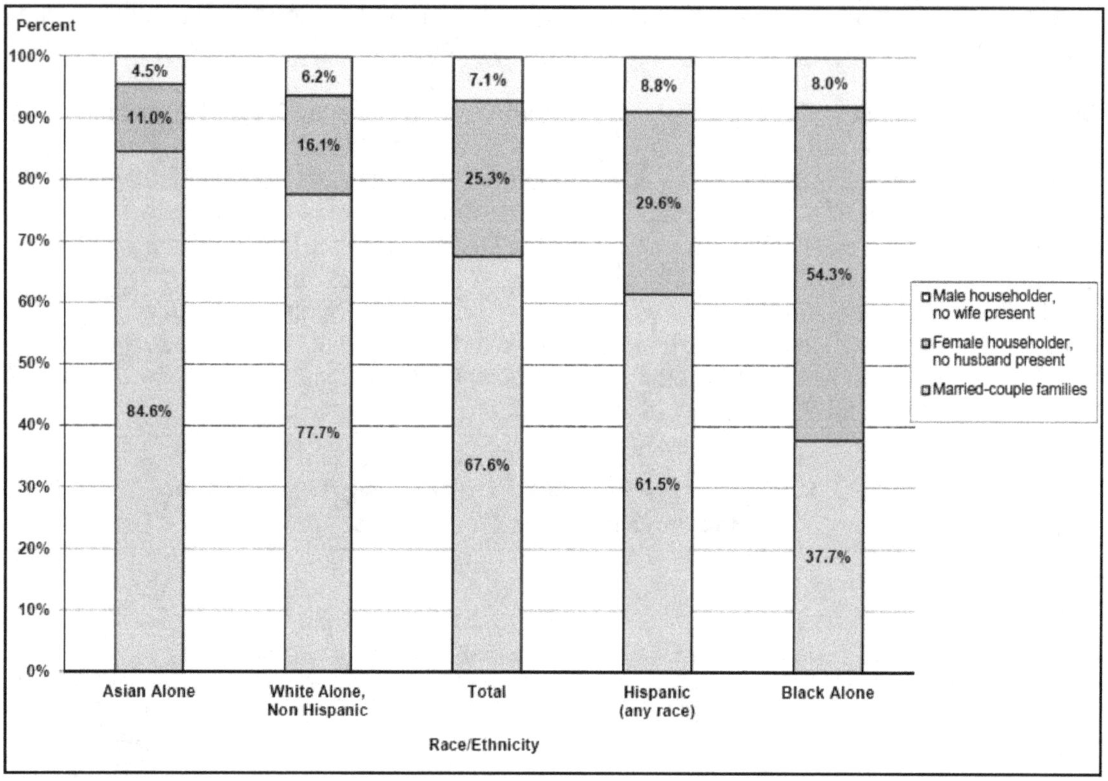

Source: Figure prepared by the Congressional Research Service (CRS) based on U.S. Census Bureau data from the 2013 Current Population Survey Annual Social and Economic Supplement, available at http://www.census.gov/hhes/www/cpstables/032013/pov/pov05_100.htm.

Adults with Low Education, Unemployment, or Disability

Adults with low education, those who are unemployed, or those who have a work-related disability are especially prone to poverty. In 2012 among 25- to 34-year-olds without a high school diploma, about 2 out of 5 (39.1%) were poor. Within the same age group, over 1 of 5 (21.5%) whose highest level of educational attainment was a high school diploma were poor. In contrast, only about 1 in 18 (5.6%) of 25- to 34-year-olds with at least a bachelor's degree were found to be living below the poverty line. (About 11% of 25- to 34-year-olds lack a high school diploma.) Among persons between the ages of 16 and 64 who were unemployed in March 2013, nearly 3 out of 10 (28.6%) were poor based on their families' incomes in 2012; among those who were employed, 7.0% were poor. In 2012, persons who had a work disability[11] represented 11.3%

[11] The CPS asks several questions to determine whether individuals are considered to have a work disability. Persons are identified as having a work disability if they (1) reported having a health problem or disability that prevents them from working or that limits the kind or amount of work they can do; (2) ever retired or left a job for health reasons; (3) did not work in the survey week because of long-term physical or mental illness or disability which prevents the performance of any kind of work; (4) did not work at all in the previous year because they were ill or disabled; (5) are under 65 years of age and covered by Medicare; (6) are under age 65 years of age and a recipient of Supplemental Security Income (SSI); or (7) received veteran's disability compensation. Persons are considered to have a severe work disability if they meet any of the criteria in (3) through (6), above. See http://www.census.gov/hhes/www/disability/disabcps html.

of the 16- to 64-year-old population, and about one-quarter (25.3%) of the poor population within this age range. Among those with a severe work disability, 34.9% were poor, compared to 16.7% of those with a less severe disability and 11.6% who reported having no work-related disability.

The Aged

In spite of the recession, the poverty rate among the aged remained at a historic low of 9.1% in 2012 (statistically tied with the 2011 rate of 8.7%). In 2012, an estimated 3.9 million persons age 65 and older were considered poor under the "official" poverty measure. Among persons age 75 and over, 10.6% were poor in 2012, compared to 7.9% of those ages 65 to 74. Many of the aged live just slightly above the poverty line. As measured by a slightly raised poverty standard (125% of the poverty threshold), 14.8% of the aged could be considered poor or "*near poor*"; 12.1% who are ages 65 to 74, and 17.8% who are 75 years of age and over, could be considered poor or "near poor."

Receipt of Need-Tested Assistance Among the Poor

In 2012, among poor persons, nearly three of every four (74.4%) lived in households that received any means-tested assistance during the year.[12] Such assistance could include cash aid, such as Temporary Assistance for Needy Families (TANF), Supplemental Security Income (SSI) payments, SNAP benefits (Food Stamps), Medicaid, subsidized housing, free or reduced price school lunches, and other programs. In 2012, fewer than 1 in 5 (18.5%) poor persons lived in households that received *cash aid*; half (50.6%) received SNAP benefits (formerly named Food Stamps); 6 in 10 (61.8%) lived in households where one or more household members were covered by Medicaid; and about 1 in 7 (14.9%) lived in subsidized housing. Poor single-parent families with children are among those families most likely to receive cash aid. Among poor children who were living in single female-headed families, one-quarter (24.0%) were in households that received government cash aid in 2012. The share of poor children in single female-headed families receiving cash aid is well below historical levels. In 1993, 70.2% of these children's families received cash aid. In 1995, the year prior to passage of sweeping welfare changes under PRWORA, 65% of such children were in families receiving cash aid.

The Geography of Poverty

Poverty is more highly concentrated in some areas than in others; it is about twice as high in center cities as it is in suburban areas and nearly three times as high in the poorest states as it is in the least poor states. Some neighborhoods may be characterized as having high concentrations of poverty. Among the poor, the likelihood of living in an area of concentrated or extreme poverty varies by race and ethnicity.

---

[12] See http://www.census.gov/hhes/www/cpstables/032013/pov/pov26_000 htm.

Poverty in Metropolitan and Nonmetropolitan Areas, Center Cities, and Suburbs

Within metropolitan areas, the incidence of poverty in central city areas is considerably higher than in suburban areas—19.7% versus 11.2%, respectively, in 2012. Nonmetropolitan areas had a poverty rate of 17.7%. A typical pattern is for poverty rates to be highest in center city areas, with poverty rates dropping off in suburban areas, and then rising with increasing distance from an urban core.

Poverty by Region

In 2012, poverty rates were lowest in the Northeast (13.6%), followed by the Midwest (13.3%), and the West (15.1%), with the South having the highest poverty rate (16.5%). Among the four regions, only the West experienced statistically significant change in its poverty rate from 2011 to 2012, with its rate declining from 15.8% to 15.1% over the period.

State Poverty Rates

American Community Survey (ACS) State Poverty Estimates—2012

Up to this point, the poverty statistics presented in this report come from the U.S. Census Bureau's Annual Social and Economic Supplement (ASEC) to the Current Population Survey (CPS). For purposes of producing state and sub-state poverty estimates, the Census Bureau now recommends using the American Community Survey (ACS)—because of its much larger sample size, the ACS produces estimates with a much smaller margin of statistical error than that of the CPS/ASEC. However, it should be noted that the ACS survey design differs from the CPS/ASEC in a variety of ways, and may produce somewhat different estimates than those obtained from the ASEC/CPS. Based on the 2012 ACS, the U.S. poverty rate was estimated to be 15.9%, compared to 15.0% based on the 2013 CPS/ASEC. The CPS/ASEC estimates are based on a survey conducted in February through April 2013, and account for income reported for the previous year. In contrast, the ACS estimates are based on income information collected between January and December 2012, for the prior 12 months. For example, for the sample with data collected in January, the reference period is from January 2011 to December 2011, and for the sample with data collected in December, from December 2011 to November 2012. The ACS data consequently cover a time span of 23 months, with the data centered at mid-December 2011.

Based on 2012 American Community Survey (ACS) data, poverty rates were highest in the South (with the exception of Virginia), extending across to Southwestern states bordering Mexico (Texas, New Mexico, and Arizona). (See **Figure 5**.) Poverty rates in several states bordering the Ohio River (Ohio, West Virginia, Kentucky) also exceeded the national rate, as did those of Michigan and the District of Columbia, in the eastern half of the nation, and California, Oregon, and Nevada in the western half.

States along the Atlantic Seaboard from Virginia northward tended to have poverty rates well below the national rate, as did three contiguous states in the upper Midwest/plains (Iowa, Minnesota, and North Dakota), as well as Utah, Wyoming, Alaska, and Hawaii.

Figure 5. Percentage of People in Poverty in the Past 12 Months by State and Puerto Rico: 2012

Source: U.S. Census Bureau, 2011 American Community Survey, 2012 Puerto Rico Community Survey. Alemayehu Bishaw, *Poverrty: 2000 to 2012*, U.S. Census Bureau, American Community Survey Briefs, ACSBR/12 01, Washington, DC, September 2013, p. 5, http://www.census.gov/prod/2013pubs/acsbr12-01.pdf

Figure 6 shows estimated poverty rates for the United States and for each of the 50 states and the District of Columbia on the basis of the 2012 American Community Survey (ACS), the most recent ACS data currently available. In addition to the point estimates, the figure displays a 90% statistical confidence interval around each state's estimate, indicating the degree to which these estimates might be expected to vary based on sample size. Although the states are sorted from lowest to highest by their respective poverty rate point estimates, the precise ranking of each state is not possible because of the depicted margin of error around each state's estimate. All states with non-overlapping statistical confidence intervals have statistically significant different poverty rates from one another. Some states with overlapping confidence intervals may also have significantly different poverty rates from one another, measured at the 90% confidence interval.[13]

[13] Two states' poverty rates are statistically different at the 90% statistical confidence interval if the confidence intervals bounding their respective poverty rates do not overlap with one another. However, some states with overlapping confidence intervals may also statistically differ at the 90% statistical confidence interval. In order to precisely determine whether two states' poverty rates differ from one another, a statistical test of differences must be performed. The standard error for the difference between two estimates may be calculated as: $SE_{StateA} - SE_{StateB} = \sqrt{SE^2_{StateA} + SE^2_{StateB}}$. Two estimates are considered statistically different if at the 90% statistical confidence interval the absolute value of the difference is greater than 1.645 times the standard error of the difference (i.e., $|Povrate_{StateA} - Povrate_{StateB}| > 1.645x(SE_{StateA} - SE_{StateB})$. Note that the standard error for a state's poverty estimate may be obtained by dividing the margin of error depicted in (continued...)

For example, New Hampshire, shown as having the lowest poverty rate (10.0%) in 2012, is statistically tied with several other states, including Alaska (10.1%), Maryland (10.3%), Connecticut (10.6%), and New Jersey (10.8%). Mississippi clearly stands out as the state with the highest poverty rate (24.2%). New Mexico, with a poverty rate of 20.8%, has the second-highest poverty rate, and is statistically untied with any other state, even though its statistical confidence interval overlaps with several other states. Louisiana, a state ranked as having the third-highest poverty rate (19.9%), is statistically tied with Arkansas (19.8%) and Kentucky (19.4%), but not with Georgia (19.2) nor Alabama (19.0), even though their statistical confidence intervals overlap.

(...continued)

Figure 6 by 1.645.

Figure 6. Poverty Rates for the 50 States and the District of Columbia: 2012 American Community Survey (ACS) Data

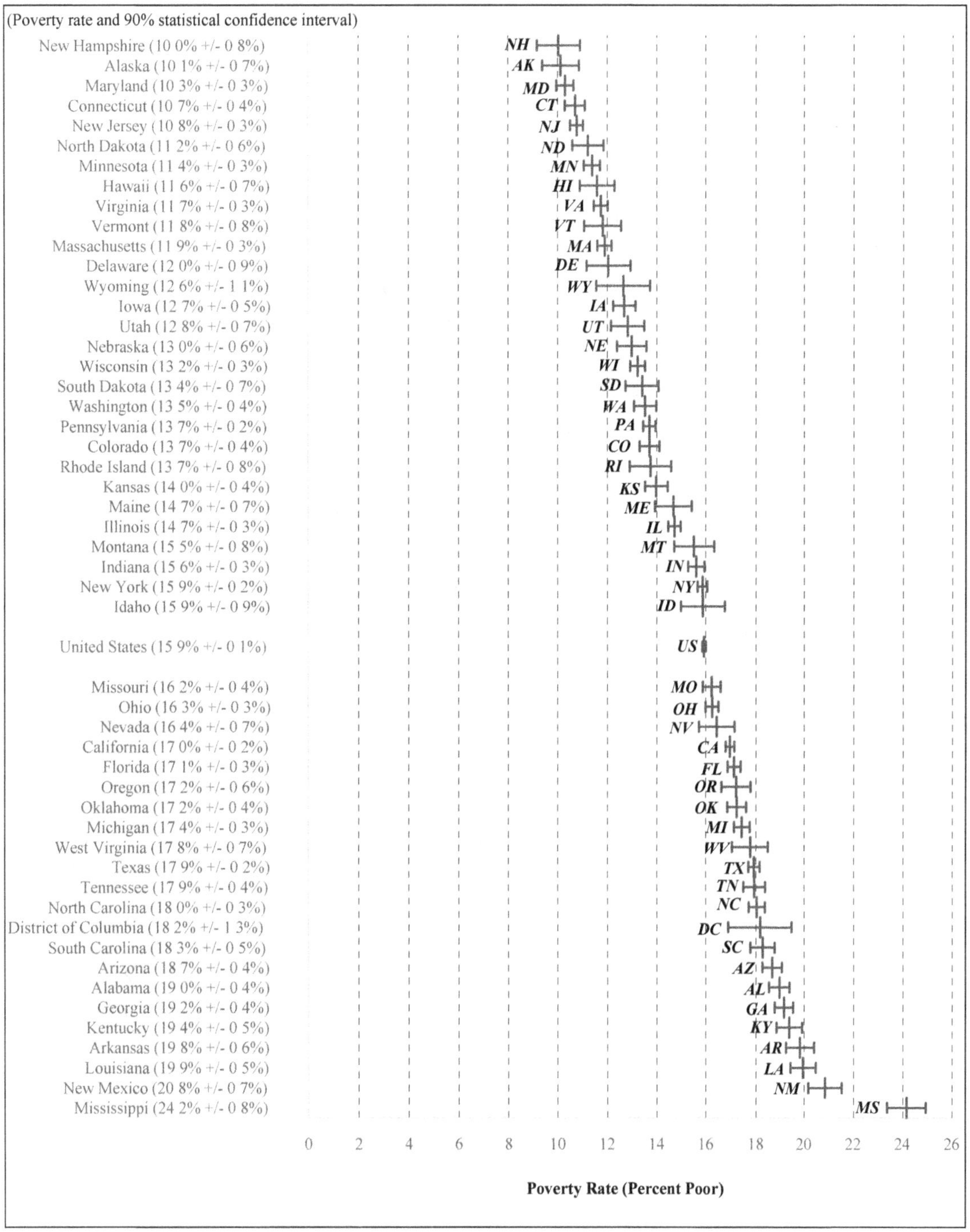

Source: Prepared by the Congressional Research Service on the basis of U.S. Census Bureau 2012 American Community Survey (ACS) data.

Change in State Poverty Rates: 2002-2012

Table 1 provides estimates of state and national poverty rates from 2002 through 2012 from the ACS. Statistically significant changes from one year to the next are indicated by an upward-pointing arrow (▲) if a state's poverty rate was statistically higher, and by a downward-pointing arrow (▼) if statistically lower, than in the immediately preceding year or for other selected periods (i.e., 2005 vs. 2002, 2011 vs. 2007).[14] It should be noted that ACS poverty estimates for 2006 and later are not strictly comparable to those of earlier years, due to a change in ACS methodology that began in 2006 to include some persons living in non-institutionalized group quarters who were not included in earlier years.[15]

Table 1 shows that three states (California, Mississippi, and New Hampshire) experienced statistically significant increases in their poverty rates from the 2011 to 2012 ACS. California's estimated poverty rate increased from 16.6% in 2011, to 17.0% in 2012, while Mississippi's rate increased from 22.6% to 24.2%, and New Hampshire's rate increased from 8.8% to 10.0%, over the period. Two states (Minnesota and Texas) experienced statistically significant decreases in their poverty rates from 2011 to 2012, with Minnesota's rate falling from 11.9% to 11.4%, and Texas's rate falling from 18.5% to 17.9% over the period.

The table shows that poverty among states generally increased over the 2002 to 2005 period, as measured by the ACS, consequent to the 2001 (March to November) economic recession. From the 2002 to 2003 ACS, five states (including the District of Columbia) experienced statistically significant increases in their poverty rates, whereas none experienced a statistically significant decrease. From 2003 to 2004, eight states saw their poverty rates increase, whereas two saw decreases. From 2004 to 2005, 13 states saw their poverty rates increase, whereas only 1 saw its poverty rate decrease. Comparing poverty rates from the 2005 ACS to those from the 2002 ACS, poverty was statistically higher in 25 states, and lower in only 2.

By 2007, poverty rates among states were beginning to improve, with 13 states (including the District of Columbia) experiencing statistically significant declines in their poverty rates from 2006; only Michigan experienced a statistically significant increase in its poverty rate in 2007 compared to a year earlier.

Since 2007, state poverty rates have generally increased consequent to the 18-month recession (December 2007 to June 2009). From 2007 to 2008, the ACS data showed eight states (California, Connecticut, Florida, Hawaii, Indiana, Michigan, Oregon, and Pennsylvania) as experiencing statistically significant increases in their poverty rates, whereas three states (Alabama, Louisiana, and Texas) experienced statistically significant decreases. From 2008 to 2009, 32 states saw their poverty rates increase, and no state experienced a statistically significant decrease, and from 2009 to 2010, 34 states experienced statistically significant increases in poverty, and again, no state

[14] Statistically significant differences are based on a 90% statistical confidence interval.

[15] Beginning in 2006, a portion of the population living in non-institutional group quarters has been included in the ACS in estimating poverty. The population living in institutional group quarters, military barracks, and college dormitories has been excluded in the ACS poverty estimates for all years. The part of the non-institutional group quarters population that has been included in the poverty universe since 2006 (e.g., people living in group homes or those living in agriculture workers' dormitories) is considerably more likely to be in poverty than people living in households. Consequently, estimates of poverty in 2006 and after are somewhat higher than would be the case if all group quarters residents were excluded—thus, comparisons with earlier year estimates are not strictly comparable.

experienced a decrease. As noted above, from 2011 to 2012, three states saw their poverty rates rise, and only two saw a decline. Comparing 2012 to 2007, poverty rates were statistically higher in 47 states (including the District of Columbia), and no state had a poverty rate statistically below its prerecession rate.

Table 1. Poverty Rates for the 50 States and the District of Columbia, 2002 to 2012 Estimates from the American Community Survey (ACS)

(percent poor)

	Estimated Poverty Rates and Statistically Significant Differences over Previous Year											Change in Poverty Rates over Selected Periods and Statistically Significant Differences[a]	
	2002	2003	2004	2005	2006[b]	2007[b]	2008[b]	2009[b]	2010[b]	2011[b]	2012[b]	2005 vs. 2001	2012 vs. 2007
United States	12.4	12.7 ▲	13.1 ▲	13.3 ▲	13.3	13.0 ▼	13.2	14.3 ▲	15.3 ▲	15.9 ▲	15.9	0.9 ▲	3.0 ▲
Alabama	16.6	17.1	16.1	17.0 ▲	16.6	16.9	15.7 ▼	17.5 ▲	19.0 ▲	19.0	19.0	-0.1	2.1 ▲
Alaska	7.7	9.7 ▲	8.2 ▼	11.2 ▲	10.9	8.9 ▼	8.4	9.0	9.9	10.5	10.1	3.2 ▲	1.2 ▲
Arizona	14.2	15.4 ▲	14.2	14.2	14.2	14.2	14.7	16.5 ▲	17.4 ▲	19.0 ▲	18.7	0.0	4.5 ▲
Arkansas	15.3	16.0	17.9 ▲	17.2	17.3	17.9	17.3	18.8 ▲	18.8	19.5	19.8	2.0 ▲	2.0 ▲
Ca ifornia	13.0	13.4	13.3	13.3	13.1	12.4 ▼	13.3 ▲	14.2 ▲	15.8 ▲	16.6 ▲	17.0 ▲	0.1	4.6 ▲
Colorado	9.7	9.8	11.1	11.1	12.0 ▲	12.0	11.4	12.9 ▲	13.4	13.5	13.7	2.3 ▲	1.7 ▲
Connecticut	7.5	8.1	7.6	8.3	8.3	7.9	9.3 ▲	9.4	10.1 ▲	10.9 ▲	10.7	0.8	2.8 ▲
Delaware	8.2	8.7	9.9	10.4	11.1	10.5	10.0	10.8	11.8	11.9	12.0	2.9 ▲	1.6 ▲
Dist. of Col.	17.5	19.9 ▲	18.9	19.0	19.6	16.4 ▼	17.2	18.4	19.2	18.7	18.2	2.2	1.7
Florida	12.8	13.1	12.2 ▼	12.8 ▲	12.6	12.1 ▼	13.2 ▲	14.9 ▲	16.5 ▲	17.0 ▲	17.1	-0.2	5.0 ▲
Georgia	12.7	13.4	14.8 ▲	14.4	14.7	14.3	14.7	16.5 ▲	17.9 ▲	19.1 ▲	19.2	2.0 ▲	4.9 ▲
Hawaii	10.1	10.9	10.6	9.8	9.3	8.0 ▼	9.1 ▲	10.4 ▲	10.7	12.0 ▲	11.6	-0.8	3.6 ▲
Idaho	13.8	13.8	14.5	13.9	12.6 ▼	12.1	12.6	14.3 ▲	15.7 ▲	16.5	15.9	-1.2	3.7 ▲
Illinois	11.6	11.3	11.9	12.0	12.3	11.9	12.2	13.3 ▲	13.8 ▲	15.0 ▲	14.7	0.7 ▲	2.8 ▲
Indiana	10.9	10.6	10.8	12.2 ▲	12.7	12.3	13.1 ▲	14.4 ▲	15.3 ▲	16.0 ▲	15.6	1.8 ▲	3.3 ▲
Iowa	11.2	10.1	9.9	10.9 ▲	11.0	11.0	11.5	11.8	12.6 ▲	12.8	12.7	-0.2	1.7 ▲
Kansas	12.1	10.8	10.5	11.7 ▲	12.4	11.2 ▼	11.3	13.4 ▲	13.6	13.8	14.0	0.3	2.8 ▲

	Estimated Poverty Rates and Statistically Significant Differences over Previous Year											Change in Poverty Rates over Selected Periods and Statistically Significant Differences[a]	
	2002	2003	2004	2005	2006[b]	2007[b]	2008[b]	2009[b]	2010[b]	2011[b]	2012[b]	2005 vs. 2001	2012 vs. 2007
Kentucky	15.6	17.4	17.4	16.8	17.0	17.3	17.3	18.6 ▲	19.0	19.1	19.4	1.3 ▲	2.1 ▲
Louisiana	18.8	20.3	19.4	19.8	19.0	18.6	17.3 ▼	17.3	18.7 ▲	20.4 ▲	19.9	0.2	1.3 ▲
Maine	11.1	10.5	12.3 ▲	12.6	12.9	12.0	12.3	12.3	12.9	14.1 ▲	14.7	1.8 ▲	2.6 ▲
Maryland	8.1	8.2	8.8	8.2	7.8	8.3	8.1	9.1 ▲	9.9 ▲	10.1	10.3	-0.3	2.0 ▲
Massachusetts	8.9	9.4	9.2	10.3 ▲	9.9	9.9	10.0	10.3	11.4 ▲	11.6	11.9	1.0 ▲	1.9 ▲
Michigan	11.0	11.4	12.3	13.2 ▲	13.5	14.0 ▲	14.4 ▲	16.2 ▲	16.8 ▲	17.5 ▲	17.4	2.5 ▲	3.4 ▲
Minnesota	8.5	7.8	8.3	9.2 ▲	9.8 ▲	9.5	9.6	11.0 ▲	11.6 ▲	11.9	11.4 ▼	1.2 ▲	1.9 ▲
Mississippi	19.9	19.9	21.6 ▲	21.3	21.1	20.6	21.2	21.9	22.4	22.6	24.2 ▲	1.2 ▲	3.5 ▲
Missouri	11.9	11.7	11.8	13.3 ▲	13.6	13.0 ▼	13.4	14.6 ▲	15.3 ▲	15.8	16.2	1.6 ▲	3.2 ▲
Montana	14.6	14.2	14.2	14.4	13.6	14.1	14.8	15.1	14.6	14.8	15.5	-1.0	1.4 ▲
Nebraska	11.0	10.8	11.0	10.9	11.5	11.2	10.8	12.3 ▲	12.9	13.1	13.0	0.5	1.8 ▲
Nevada	11.8	11.5	12.6	11.1	10.3	10.7	11.3	12.4 ▲	14.9 ▲	15.9	16.4	-1.5 ▼	5.8 ▲
New Hampshire	6.4	7.7 ▲	7.6	7.5	8.0	7.1 ▼	7.6	8.5 ▲	8.3	8.8	10.0 ▲	1.6 ▲	3.0 ▲
New Jersey	7.5	8.4 ▲	8.5	8.7	8.7	8.6	8.7	9.4 ▲	10.3 ▲	10.4	10.8	1.2 ▲	2.2 ▲
New Mexico	18.9	18.6	19.3	18.5	18.5	18.1	17.1	18.0	20.4 ▲	21.5	20.8	-0.4	2.7 ▲
New York	13.1	13.5	14.2 ▲	13.8	14.2 ▲	13.7 ▼	13.6	14.2 ▲	14.9 ▲	16.0 ▲	15.9	1.1 ▲	2.2 ▲
North Carolina	14.2	14.0	15.2	15.1	14.7	14.3	14.6	16.3 ▲	17.5 ▲	17.9	18.0	0.4	3.7 ▲
North Dakota	12.5	11.7	12.1	11.2	11.4	12.1	12.0	11.7	13.0 ▲	12.2	11.2	-1.1	-0.9
Ohio	11.9	12.1	12.5	13.0	13.3	13.1	13.4	15.2 ▲	15.8 ▲	16.4 ▲	16.3	1.5 ▲	3.1 ▲
Oklahoma	15.0	16.1	15.3	16.5	17.0	15.9 ▼	15.9	16.2	16.9 ▲	17.2	17.2	2.0 ▲	1.3 ▲
Oregon	13.2	13.9	14.1	14.1	13.3 ▼	12.9	13.6 ▲	14.3	15.8 ▲	17.5 ▲	17.2	0.0	4.3 ▲

	Estimated Poverty Rates and Statistically Significant Differences over Previous Year											Change in Poverty Rates over Selected Periods and Statistically Significant Differences[a]	
												2005 vs. 2001	2012 vs. 2007
	2002	2003	2004	2005	2006[b]	2007[b]	2008[b]	2009[b]	2010[b]	2011[b]	2012[b]		
Pennsylvania	10.5	10.9	11.7 ▲	11.9	12.1	11.6 ▼	12.1 ▲	12.5 ▲	13.4 ▲	13.8	13.7	1.5 ▲	2.1 ▲
Rhode Island	10.7	11.3	12.8 ▲	12.3	11.1	12.0	11.7	11.5	14.0 ▲	14.7	13.7	0.4	1.8 ▲
South Carolina	14.2	14.1	15.7	15.6	15.7	15.0	15.7	17.1 ▲	18.2 ▲	18.9 ▲	18.3	1.4 ▲	3.2 ▲
South Dakota	11.4	11.1	11.0	13.6 ▲	13.6	13.1	12.5	14.2 ▲	14.4	13.9	13.4	2.2	0.3
Tennessee	14.5	13.8	14.5	15.5	16.2	15.9	15.5	17.1 ▲	17.7	18.3	17.9	1.7 ▲	2.0 ▲
Texas	15.6	16.3	16.6	17.6 ▲	16.9 ▼	16.3 ▼	15.8 ▼	17.2 ▲	17.9 ▲	18.5 ▲	17.9 ▼	1.3 ▲	1.6 ▲
Utah	10.5	10.6	10.9	10.2	10.6	9.7 ▼	9.6	11.5 ▲	13.2 ▲	13.5	12.8	0.1	3.2 ▲
Vermont	8.5	9.7	9.0	11.5 ▲	10.3	10.1	10.6	11.4	12.7 ▲	11.5 ▼	11.8	1.8 ▲	1.7 ▲
Virginia	9.9	9.0	9.5	10.0	9.6	9.9	10.2	10.5	11.1 ▲	11.5 ▲	11.7	-0.4	1.8 ▲
Washington	11.4	11.0	13.1 ▲	11.9 ▼	11.8	11.4	11.3	12.3 ▲	13.4 ▲	13.9	13.5	0.4	2.1 ▲
West Virginia	17.2	18.5	17.9	18.0	17.3	16.9	17.0	17.7	18.1	18.6	17.8	0.1	0.9
Wisconsin	9.7	10.5	10.7	10.2	11.0 ▲	10.8	10.4	12.4 ▲	13.2 ▲	13.1	13.2	1.2 ▲	2.4 ▲
Wyoming	11.0	9.7	10.3	9.5	9.4	8.7	9.4	9.8	11.2	11.3	12.6	-1.6 ▼	4.0 ▲
Number of states with statistically significant change in poverty:		5	10	14	7	14	11	32	34	18	5	27	47
Increase in poverty		5 ▲	8 ▲	13 ▲	4 ▲	1 ▲	8 ▲	32 ▲	34 ▲	17 ▲	3	25 ▲	47 ▲
Decrease in poverty		0 ▼	2 ▼	1 ▼	3 ▼	13 ▼	3 ▼	0 ▼	0 ▼	1 ▼	2	2 ▼	0 ▼

Source: Congressional Research Service (CRS) estimates from U.S. Census Bureau American Community Survey (ACS) data, 2002 to 2012.

Notes: ▲ Statistically significant increase in poverty rate at the 90% statistical confidence level.

▼ Statistically significant decrease in poverty rate at the 90% statistical confidence level.

a. Depicted changes in poverty rates over selected periods may differ slightly from differences calculated directly from the table, due to rounding.

b. Comparisons to 2002 through 2005 estimates are not strictly comparable, due to inclusion of persons living in some non-institutional group quarters beginning in 2006 and after.

Poverty Rates by Metropolitan Area

The four tables that follow provide poverty estimates for large metropolitan areas having a population of 500,000 and over, and for smaller metropolitan areas having a population of 50,000 or more but less than 500,000. Among large metropolitan areas, 10 areas with some of the lowest poverty rates are shown in **Table 2**, and the 10 areas with some of the highest poverty rates are shown in **Table 3**. Among smaller metropolitan areas, 10 areas with some of the lowest poverty rates are shown in **Table 4**, and 10 among those with the highest poverty rates in **Table 5**. It should be noted that metropolitan areas shown in these tables may not be statistically different from one another, or from others not shown in the tables.

Poverty estimates for all metropolitan areas are shown in **Appendix B**. **Table B-1** includes poverty rate estimates for 2012, and whether 2012 estimates statistically differ from 2011. The table shows that from 2011 to 2012, 26 metropolitan areas experienced statistically significant increases in their poverty rates, whereas 25 areas experienced statistically significant decreases.

Table 2. Large Metropolitan Areas Among Those with the Lowest Poverty Rates: 2012

(Metropolitan Areas with Population of 500,000 and Over)

		Number Poor		Poverty Rate (Percent Poor)	
Metropolitan Area	**Total Population**	**Estimate**	**Margin of Error[a]**	**Estimate**	**Margin of Error[a]**
Washington-Arlington-Alexandria, DC-VA-MD-WV	5,702,639	477,661	+/-17,577	8.4%	+/-0.3%
Bridgeport-Stamford-Norwalk, CT	915,813	81,629	+/-7,143	8.9%	+/-0.8%
Ogden-Clearfield, UT	556,266	56,638	+/-7,028	10.2%	+/-1.3%
Honolulu, HI	945,975	97,754	+/-8,616	10.3%	+/-0.9%
Allentown-Bethlehem-Easton, PA-NJ	804,602	84,127	+/-6,553	10.5%	+/-0.8%
Boston-Cambridge-Quincy, MA-NH	4,486,468	479,126	+/-15,238	10.7%	+/-0.3%
Minneapolis-St. Paul-Bloomington, MN-WI	3,299,784	352,560	+/-14,086	10.7%	+/-0.4%
San Jose-Sunnyvale-Santa Clara, CA	1,868,187	202,357	+/-12,662	10.8%	+/-0.7%
Hartford-West Hartford-East Hartford, CT	1,169,356	127,371	+/-7,291	10.9%	+/-0.6%
Albany-Schenectady-Troy, NY	843,802	93,228	+/-6,350	11.0%	+/-0.8%

Source: Table prepared by the Congressional Research Service (CRS) based on analysis of U.S. Census Bureau 2012 American Community Survey (ACS) data, table series S1701: Poverty Status in the Past 12 Months, from the Census Bureau's American FactFinder, available at http://factfinder2.census.gov/faces/nav/jsf/pages/index.xhtml.

Notes: Areas are included based on their estimated 2012 poverty rates. Areas shown may not be statistically different from one another, or from others not shown in the table.

a. Margin of error of an estimate based on a 90% statistical confidence level. When added to and subtracted from an estimate, the range reflects a 90% statistical confidence interval bounding the estimate.

Table 3. Large Metropolitan Areas Among Those with the Highest Poverty Rates: 2012

(Metropolitan Areas with Population of 500,000 and Over)

Metropolitan Area	Total Population	Number Poor		Poverty Rate (Percent Poor)	
		Estimate	Margin of Error[a]	Estimate	Margin of Error[a]
McAllen-Edinburg-Mission, TX	796,479	274,713	+/-17,146	34.5%	+/-2.2%
Fresno, CA	930,872	264,738	+/-13,321	28.4%	+/-1.4%
El Paso, TX	812,645	195,247	+/-10,809	24.0%	+/-1.3%
Bakersfield-Delano, CA	825,020	196,625	+/-13,837	23.8%	+/-1.7%
Jackson, MS	531,354	117,984	+/-8,520	22.2%	+/-1.6%
Modesto, CA	515,955	104,559	+/-10,039	20.3%	+/-1.9%
Augusta-Richmond County, GA-SC	553,981	112,218	+/-8,963	20.3%	+/-1.6%
Tucson, AZ	968,447	193,466	+/-11,146	20.0%	+/-1.1%
Toledo, OH	630,598	125,508	+/-7,513	19.9%	+/-1.2%
Memphis, TN-MS-AR	1,307,830	259,780	+/-10,892	19.9%	+/-0.8%

Source: Table prepared by the Congressional Research Service (CRS) based on analysis of U.S. Census Bureau 2012 American Community Survey (ACS) data, table series S1701: Poverty Status in the Past 12 Months, from the Census Bureau's American FactFinder, available at http://factfinder2.census.gov/faces/nav/jsf/pages/index.xhtml.

Notes: Areas are included based on their estimated 2012 poverty rates. Areas shown may not be statistically different from one another, or from others not shown in the table.

a. Margin of error of an estimate based on a 90% statistical confidence level. When added to and subtracted from an estimate, the range reflects a 90% statistical confidence interval bounding the estimate.

Table 4. Smaller Metropolitan Areas Among Those with the Lowest Poverty Rates: 2012

(Metropolitan Areas with Populations Between 50,000 and 499,999)

Metropolitan Area	Total Population	Number Poor		Poverty Rate (Percent Poor)	
		Estimate	Margin of Error[a]	Estimate	Margin of Error[a]
Midland, TX	145,188	9,086	+/-2,649	6.3%	+/-1.8%
Bismarck, ND	110,290	7,266	+/-1,572	6.6%	+/-1.4%
Fairbanks, AK	96,529	6,646	+/-1,813	6.9%	+/-1.9%
Appleton, WI	225,045	18,885	+/-2,630	8.4%	+/-1.2%
Anchorage, AK	384,749	33,353	+/-4,104	8.7%	+/-1.1%
Fond du Lac, WI	98,703	8,608	+/-1,938	8.7%	+/-2.0%
Napa, CA	135,439	11,996	+/-2,747	8.9%	+/-2.0%

Ocean City, NJ	93,825	8,392	+/-2,201	8.9%	+/-2.3%
Norwich-New London, CT	262,896	24,105	+/-3,537	9.2%	+/-1.3%
Cedar Rapids, IA	254,225	24,150	+/-3,246	9.5%	+/-1.3%

Source: Table prepared by the Congressional Research Service (CRS) based on analysis of U.S. Census Bureau 2012 American Community Survey (ACS) data, table series S1701: Poverty Status in the Past 12 Months, from the Census Bureau's American FactFinder, available at http://factfinder2.census.gov/faces/nav/jsf/pages/index.xhtml.

Notes: Areas are included based on their estimated 2012 poverty rates. Areas shown may not be statistically different from one another, or from others not shown in the table.

a. Margin of error of an estimate based on a 90% statistical confidence level. When added to and subtracted from an estimate, the range reflects a 90% statistical confidence interval bounding the estimate.

Table 5. Smaller Metropolitan Areas Among Those with the Highest Poverty Rates: 2012

(Metropolitan Areas with Population of 500,000 and Over)

		Number Poor		Poverty Rate (Percent Poor)	
Metropolitan Area	**Total Population**	**Estimate**	**Margin of Error[a]**	**Estimate**	**Margin of Error[a]**
Brownsville-Harlingen, TX	411,003	148,267	+/-9,666	36.1%	+/-2.3%
Laredo, TX	254,758	81,651	+/-7,394	32.1%	+/-2.9%
Visalia-Porterville, CA	444,186	135,194	+/-9,353	30.4%	+/-2.1%
Gainesville, FL	254,375	70,552	+/-5,754	27.7%	+/-2.2%
Las Cruces, NM	209,622	56,903	+/-6,722	27.1%	+/-3.2%
Albany, GA	148,869	40,011	+/-4,170	26.9%	+/-2.8%
College Station-Bryan, TX	219,226	57,006	+/-5,130	26.0%	+/-2.3%
Flagstaff, AZ	127,795	33,191	+/-4,344	26.0%	+/-3.4%
Monroe, LA	168,014	43,435	+/-5,407	25.9%	+/-3.2%
Hattiesburg, MS	143,389	36,577	+/-4,869	25.5%	+/-3.4%

Source: Table prepared by the Congressional Research Service (CRS) based on analysis of U.S. Census Bureau 2012 American Community Survey (ACS) data, table series S1701: Poverty Status in the Past 12 Months, from the Census Bureau's American FactFinder, available at http://factfinder2.census.gov/faces/nav/jsf/pages/index.xhtml.

Notes: Areas are included based on their estimated 2012 poverty rates. Areas shown may not be statistically different from one another, or from others not shown in the table.

a. Margin of error of an estimate based on a 90% statistical confidence level. When added to and subtracted from an estimate, the range reflects a 90% statistical confidence interval bounding the estimate.

Congressional District Poverty Estimates

Poverty estimates for congressional districts are shown in **Appendix C**. **Table C-1** includes poverty rate estimates for 2012. Congressional districts in 2012 are not directly comparable to earlier years, due to re-districting.

"Neighborhood" Poverty—Poverty Areas and Areas of Concentrated and Extreme Poverty

The estimates presented here are based on five years of American Community Survey (ACS) data (2006-2010 ACS), and will be updated once the Census Bureau releases 5-year ACS estimates for 2008-2012, in December 2013.

Neighborhoods can be delineated from U.S. Census Bureau census tracts. Census tracts usually have between 2,500 and 8,000 persons and, when first delineated, are designed to be homogeneous with respect to population characteristics, economic status, and living conditions. The Census Bureau defines "poverty areas" as census tracts having poverty rates of 20% or more.

Figure 7 groups census tracts according to their level of poverty. The first two groupings are based on poor persons living in census tracts with poverty rates below the national average (13.8% based on the five-year ACS data), and from 13.8% to less than 20.0%. Poor persons living in census tracts with poverty rates of 20% or more meet the Census Bureau definition of living in "poverty areas." Poverty areas are further demarcated in terms of poor persons living in areas of "concentrated" poverty (i.e., census tracts with poverty rates of 30% to 39.9%), and areas of "extreme" poverty (i.e., census tracts with poverty rates of 40% or more). The figure is based on five years of data (2006–2010) from the U.S. Census Bureau's American Community Survey (ACS). Five years of data are required in order to get reasonably reliable statistical data at the census tract level while at the same time preserving the confidentiality of survey respondents.

Figure 7. Distribution of Poor People by Race and Hispanic Origin, by Level of Neighborhood (Census Tract) Poverty, 2006-2010

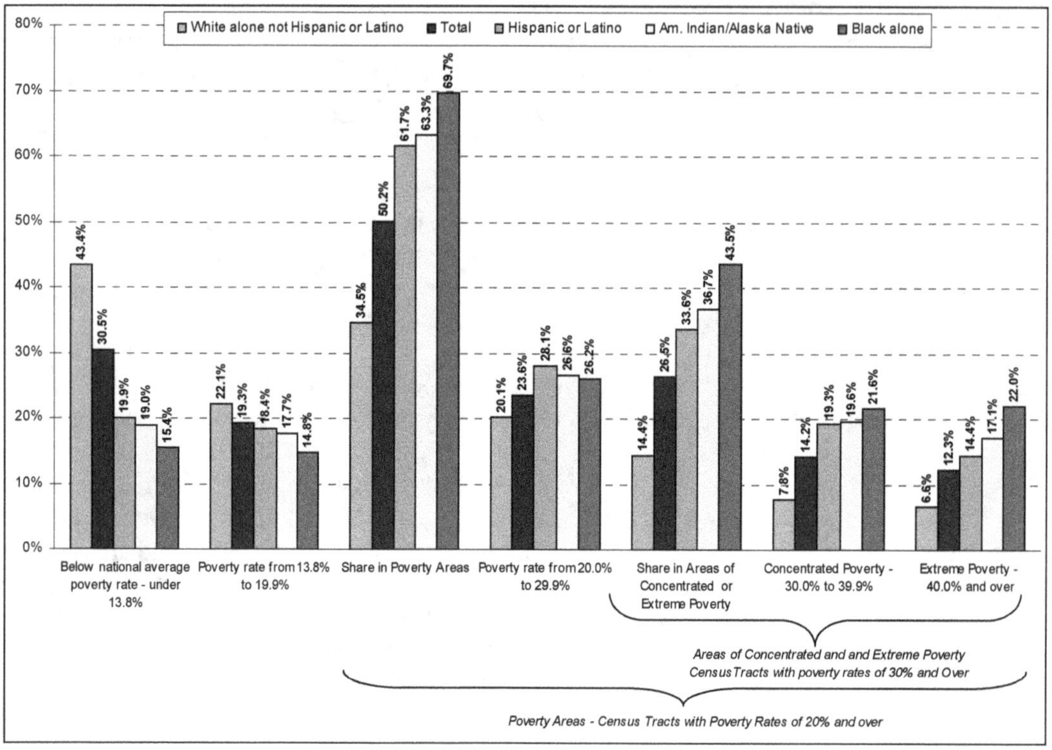

Source: Congressional Research Service (CRS) analysis of U.S. Census Bureau American Community Survey, five-year (2006-2010) data.

Figure 7 shows that over the five-year period 2006–2010, half of all poor persons (50.2%) lived in "poverty areas" (i.e., census tracts with poverty rates of 20% or more). Over one-quarter (26.5%) lived in areas with poverty of 30% or more, and about one in eight (12.3%) lived in areas of "extreme" poverty, having poverty rates of 40% or more. Among the poor, African Americans, American Indian and Alaska Natives, and Hispanics are more likely to live in poverty areas than either Asians or white non-Hispanics. Among poor blacks, over two of every five (43.5%) live in neighborhoods with poverty rates of 30% or more, and over one in five (22.0%) live in "extreme" poverty areas, with poverty rates of 40% or more. Among Hispanics, one-third (33.6%) live in areas with poverty rates of 30% or more, and about one in seven (14.4%) live in areas of "extreme" poverty. Among white non-Hispanics, close to two-thirds (64.5%) live outside poverty areas, while about one in seven (14.4%) live in areas with poverty rates of 30% or more.

The Research Supplemental Poverty Measure

On November 6, 2013, the Census Bureau released its third annual report using a new Supplemental Poverty Measure (SPM).[16] As its name implies, the SPM is intended to "supplement," rather than replace, the "official" poverty measure. The "official" Census Bureau

[16] Kathleen Short, *The Research SUPPLEMENTAL POVERTY MEASURE: 2011*, U.S. Census Bureau, P60-244, Washington, DC, November 2012, http://www.census.gov/prod/2012pubs/p60-244.pdf.

statistical measure of poverty will continue to be used by programs that allocate funds to states or other jurisdictions on the basis of poverty, and the Department of Health and Human Services (HHS) will continue to derive Poverty Income Guidelines from the "official" Census Bureau measure.

Many experts consider the "official" poverty measure to be flawed and outmoded.[17] In 1990, Congress commissioned a study on how poverty is measured in the United States, resulting in the National Academy of Sciences (NAS) convening a 12-member expert panel to study the issue. The NAS panel issued a wide range of specific recommendations to develop an improved statistical measure of poverty in its 1995 report *Measuring Poverty: A New Approach.*[18]

In late 2009, the Office of Management and Budget (OMB) formed an Interagency Technical Working Group[19] (ITWG) to suggest how the Census Bureau, in cooperation with the Bureau of Labor Statistics (BLS), should develop a new Supplemental Poverty Measure, using the NAS expert panel's recommendations as a starting point. Referencing the work of the ITWG,[20] the Department of Commerce announced in March 2010 that the Census Bureau was developing a new Supplemental Poverty Measure, as "an alternative lens to understand poverty and measure the effects of anti-poverty policies," with the intention that the new measure "will be dynamic and will benefit from improvements over time based on new data and new methodologies."[21]

The SPM is intended to address a number of weaknesses of the "official" measure. Criticisms of the "official" poverty measure raised by the NAS expert panel include the following:

- *The "official" poverty measure, by counting only families' total cash, pre-tax income as a resource in determining poverty status, ignores a host of government programs and policies that affect the disposable income families may actually have available.* For example, the official measure ignores the effects of payroll taxes paid by families, and tax benefits they may receive such as the EITC and the Child Tax Credit. It ignores a variety of in-kind benefits, such as SNAP benefits and free or reduced-price lunches under the National School Lunch Program, that free up resources to meet other needs. Similarly, it ignores housing subsidies that help make housing more affordable.
- *The "official" poverty income thresholds used in determining families' and individuals' poverty status, devised in the early 1960s, have changed little since.* Except for minor technical changes and adjustments for price inflation, poverty income thresholds have essentially been frozen in time, reflecting living standards of a half-century ago.

---

[17] For a discussion of the history and development of the U.S. poverty measure, and efforts to improve poverty measurement, see CRS Report R41187, *Poverty Measurement in the United States: History, Current Practice, and Proposed Changes*, by Thomas Gabe.

[18] National Research Council, Panel on Poverty and Family Assistance, "Measuring Poverty: A New Approach," Constance F. Citro and Robert T. Michael, eds. (Washington, DC: National Academy Press, 1995). (Hereinafter cited as Citro and Michael, *Measuring Poverty...*)

[19] The working group included representatives from BLS, the Census Bureau, the Council of Economic Advisors, the Department of Commerce, the Department of Health and Human Services, and OMB.

[20] The ITWG's guidance is available at http://www.census.gov/hhes/www/poverty/SPM_TWGObservations.pdf

[21] *Census Bureau to Develop Supplemental Poverty Measure*, March 2, 2010 News Release, Economics and Statistics Administration, U.S. Department of Commerce. Available on the Internet at http://www.esa.doc.gov/news/2010/03/02/census-bureau-develop-supplemental-poverty-measure.

- *The "official" poverty measure does not take into account necessary work-related expenses, such as child care and transportation costs that are associated with getting to work.* Child care expenses are much more common today than when the "official" poverty measure was originally developed, as mothers' labor force participation has since increased.
- *The "official" poverty measure does not take into account medical expenses that individuals and families may incur, affecting their ability to meet other basic needs.* These costs, which tend to vary by age, health status, and insurance coverage of individuals, may differentially affect families' abilities to meet other basic needs, especially given rising health care costs.
- *The "official" poverty measure does not take into account changing family situations, such as cohabitation among unmarried couples, or child support payments.*
- *The "official" poverty measure does not adjust for differences in prices across geographic areas, which may affect the cost of living from one area to another.*

The ITWG, using the NAS-panel recommendations as a starting point, suggested an approach to developing the SPM that addressed how income thresholds should be set and resources counted in measuring poverty. Conceptual differences between the "official" and supplemental poverty measures are summarized in **Table 6**.

Table 6. Poverty Measure Concepts Under "Official" and Supplemental Measures

	"Official" Poverty Measure	Supplemental Poverty Measure
Measurement units	Families and unrelated individuals	All related individuals who live at the same address, including any co-resident unrelated children who are cared for by the family (such as foster children) and any cohabitors and their children
Poverty threshold	Three times the cost of a minimum food diet in 1963	A range around the 33rd percentile (i.e., 30th to 36th percentile) of expenditures on food, shelter, clothing, and utilities (FCSU) for consumer units with exactly two children multiplied by 1.2 to account for other family needs (e.g., household supplies, personal care, non-transportation-related expenses) Based on data from the U.S. Bureau of Labor Statistics Consumer Expenditure Survey (BLS CE) Separate thresholds developed for - homeowners with a mortgage, - homeowners without a mortgage, - renters

	"Official" Poverty Measure	Supplemental Poverty Measure
Threshold adjustments	Vary by family size, composition, and age of householder	A three parameter equivalence scale for number of adults and children in the family Geographic adjustments for differences in housing costs
Updating thresholds	Consumer Price Index for Urban Consumers (CPI-U) based on all items	Five-year moving average of expenditures on FCSU from the BLS CE
Resource measures	Gross before-tax cash income	Sum of cash income **Plus** in-kind benefits that families can use to meet their FCSU needs: • Supplemental Nutritional Assistance (SNAP) • National School Lunch Program • Supplementary Nutrition Program for Women, Infants, and Children (WIC) • Housing Subsidies • Low-Income Home Energy Assistance (LIHEAP) **Plus** refundable tax credits: • Earned Income Tax Credit (EITC) • Refundable portion of the Child Tax Credit (CTC), known as the Additional Child Tax Credit (ACTC) **Minus** nondiscretionary expenses: • federal and state income taxes • payroll taxes • work-related expenses, including work-related child care expenses • medical out-of-pocket expenses (MOOP), including insurance premiums paid • child support paid

Source: Congressional Research Service (CRS). Adapted from Kathleen Short, The *Research SUPPLEMENTAL POVERTY MEASURE: 2011*, U.S. Census Bureau, P60-244, Washington, DC, November 2012, http://www.census.gov/prod/2012pubs/p60-244.pdf.

The SPM incorporates a more comprehensive income/resource definition than that used by the "official" poverty measure, including in-kind benefits (e.g., SNAP) and refundable tax credits (e.g., EITC). It also expands upon the traditional family definition based on blood, marriage, and adoption to include cohabiting partners and their family relatives as part of a broader economic unit for assessing poverty status. The SPM subtracts necessary expenses (i.e., taxes, work-related expenses including child-care, child support paid, medical out-of-pocket [MOOP] expenses) from resources to arrive at a measure of an economic unit's disposable income/resources that may be applied to a standard of need based on food, clothing, shelter, and utilities (FCSU), plus "a little bit more" for everything else. The SPM income/resource thresholds are initially set at a range in the distribution (30th to 36th percentile) of what reference families (families with exactly two children) actually spend on FCSU. Separate thresholds are derived for homeowners with a mortgage and those without a mortgage, and for renters. Thresholds are adjusted for price differences in housing costs by geographic area (metropolitan and nonmetropolitan areas in a state). Thresholds for economic units other than initial reference units (i.e., those with exactly two children) are adjusted upwards or downwards for the number of adults and number of children in the unit.

Poverty Thresholds

As described earlier, the "official" U.S. poverty measure measures cash—pre-tax—income against income thresholds that vary by family size and composition. The thresholds were derived from research that showed that the average U.S. family spent one-third of its pre-tax income on food, based on a USDA 1955 Food Consumption Survey. After pricing minimally adequate food plans for families of varying sizes and compositions, poverty thresholds were derived by multiplying the cost of those food plans by a factor of three (i.e., one-third of the thresholds were assumed to address families' food needs, and two-thirds addressed everything else). The thresholds, established in 1963, are adjusted each year for price inflation.

SPM Poverty Thresholds

The SPM poverty thresholds are based on the NAS panel recommendation that thresholds be based on a point in the empirical distribution that "reference" families spend on food, clothing, shelter, and utilities (FCSU). Based on ITWG's suggestions, the Census Bureau derives FCSU thresholds for "reference" units with exactly two children, between the 30th and 36th percentile of what such units spend on FCSU, averaged over five years of survey data from the BLS Consumer Expenditure (CE) Survey.[22] Whereas "official" poverty thresholds are based on initial thresholds adjusted for price changes over time, the SPM thresholds are based on changes in reference consumer units' actual spending on FCSU over time.

Following the ITWG's suggestion, three separate sets of thresholds are established: one set for homeowners with a mortgage, another set for homeowners without a mortgage, and a third set for renters. Following NAS panel recommendations, the ITWG suggested that initial poverty thresholds based on FCSU be multiplied by a factor of 1.2, to account for all other needs (e.g., household supplies, personal care, non-work-related transportation).[23] Additionally, thresholds are adjusted upward and downward based on SPM reference unit size using a three parameter equivalence scale based on the number of adults and children in the unit.

[22] The NAS panel recommended that the reference family for establishing initial thresholds be based on families with two adults and two children. The ITWG suggested that initial thresholds be based on consumer units with exactly two children, as children reside in a variety of family types (such as single parent families, presence of one or more grandparents, and families with cohabiting adult partners). The NAS panel recommended that initial thresholds be established at between 78% and 83% of median expenditures on FCSU of reference families, which empirically ranged between the 30th and 35th percentiles. The ITWG suggested that initial thresholds be set at a range around the 33rd percentile of expenditures on FCSU for the reference consumer units. The ITWC suggested that five years of CE data be used in establishing thresholds to smooth the change in the thresholds from one year to the next.

[23] The 1.2 multiplier applied to FCSU equals the midpoint of the NAS panel's recommended multiplier of between 1.15 and 1.25.

Lastly, the thresholds are adjusted to account for variation in geographic price differences across metropolitan and nonmetropolitan areas, by state, based on differences in median housing costs across areas relative to the nation. The geographic housing cost adjustment is applied to the shelter portion of the FCSU-based thresholds.

Figure 8 depicts poverty threshold levels under the "official" poverty measure and under the Research SPM for a resource unit consisting of two adults and two children. The figure shows that in 2012, the official poverty threshold for a family with two adults and two children was $23,283. In comparison, for a similar family, the SPM poverty threshold for homeowners with a mortgage was $25,784, $2,501 (10.7%) *above* the official poverty threshold, and for homeowners without a mortgage, $21,400, or $1,883 (8.1%) *below* the official threshold. The SPM poverty threshold for renters was $25,105 or $1,883 (7.8%), *above* the official measure.

Figure 8. Poverty Thresholds Under the "Official" Measure and the Research Supplemental Poverty Measure for Units with Two Adults and Two Children: 2012

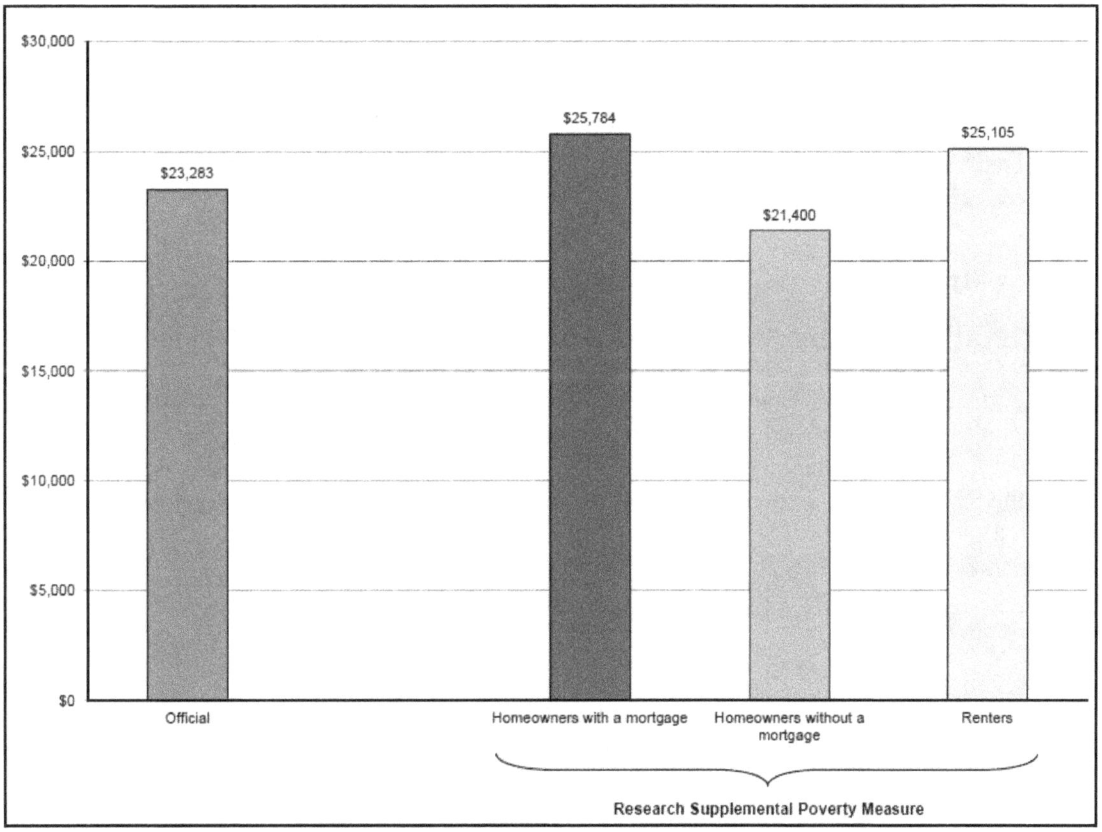

Source: Figure prepared by the Congressional Research Service (CRS), based on Kathleen Short, *The Research SUPPLEMENTAL POVERTY MEASURE: 2012*, U.S. Census Bureau, P60-247, Washington, DC, November 2013 http://www.census.gov/prod/2013pubs/p60-247.pdf.

Resources and Expenses Included in the SPM

As discussed earlier, the "official" poverty measure is based on counting families' and unrelated individuals' pre-tax cash income against poverty thresholds that vary by family size and composition. The SPM expands upon the pre-tax cash income resource definition used by the "official" measure to develop a more comprehensive measure of "disposable" income that SPM units might use to help meet basic needs (i.e., poverty thresholds based on FCSU, plus "a little more"). The SPM resource measure includes the value of a number of federal in-kind benefits, such as Supplemental Nutrition Assistance Program (SNAP, formerly Food Stamp) benefits; free and reduced-price school lunches; nutrition assistance for women, infants, and children (WIC); federal housing assistance; and energy assistance under the Low Income Home Energy Assistance Program (LIHEAP). It also includes federal tax benefits administered by the Internal Revenue Service, such as the Earned Income Tax Credit (EITC) and the partially refundable portion of the Child Tax Credit (CTC), known as the Additional Child Tax Credit (ACTC).

The SPM subtracts a number of necessary expenses from SPM units' resources to arrive at a measure of "disposable" income that units might have available to meet basic needs. Necessary expenses subtracted from resources on the SPM include child support paid; estimated federal, state, and local income taxes; estimated social security payroll (FICA) taxes; estimated work-related expenses other than child care (e.g., work-related commuting costs, purchase of uniforms or tools required for work); reported work-related child care expenses; and reported medical out of pocket (MOOP) expenses, including the employee share of health insurance premiums plus other medically necessary items such as prescription drugs and doctor copayments.

The effects of counting each of these resources and expenses in the SPM are assessed later in this report (see "Marginal Effects of Counting Specified Resources and Expenses on Poverty Under the SPM").

Poverty Estimates Under the Research SPM Compared to the "Official" Measure

In 2012, the overall poverty rate was somewhat higher under the SPM (16.0%), compared to 15.1% under an "official" poverty measure "adjusted" to include unrelated children typically excluded from the "official" measure.[24] In 2012, an estimated 49.7 million people were poor under the SPM; 2.7 million people more than the 47.0 million estimated under the "official" (adjusted) poverty measure. The remainder of this report focuses on differences in poverty rates among and between various groups under the two measures.

Poverty by Age

The SPM yields a very different impression of the incidence of poverty with respect to age than that portrayed by the "official" measure. **Figure 9** compares poverty rates by age group under the SPM and the "official" measure in 2012. The poverty rate for adults ages 18 to 64 is somewhat higher under the SPM than under the "official" measure (15.5% compared to 13.7%). The figure shows that the poverty rate for children (under age 18) is lower under the SPM than under the "official" measure (18.0% compared to 22.3%). In contrast, the poverty rate among persons age 65 and over is much higher under the SPM than under the "official" measure (14.8% compared to

[24] "Official" published estimates of poverty exclude unrelated children under the age of 15 in the universe for whom poverty is determined. For comparison with the SPM measure, these children are included in both the "adjusted official" poverty measure and the SPM. Under the "official" published poverty measure, the overall poverty rate was 15.0% in 2012; under the adjusted measure shown in this report, the overall "official" poverty rate in 2012 was 15.1%.

9.1%). Although the child poverty rate is lower under the SPM than under the "official" measure, and the aged poverty rate is considerably higher, the incidence of poverty among children still exceeds that of the aged under the SPM, as it did under the "official" measure. The SPM paints a much different picture of poverty among the aged than that conveyed by the "official" measure. As will be shown later, much of the difference between the aged poverty rate measured under the SPM compared to the "official" measure is attributable to the effect of medical expenses on the disposable income among aged units to meet basic needs represented by the SPM resource thresholds.

Figure 9. Poverty Rates Under the "Official"* and Research Supplemental Poverty Measures, by Age: 2012

(Percent poor)

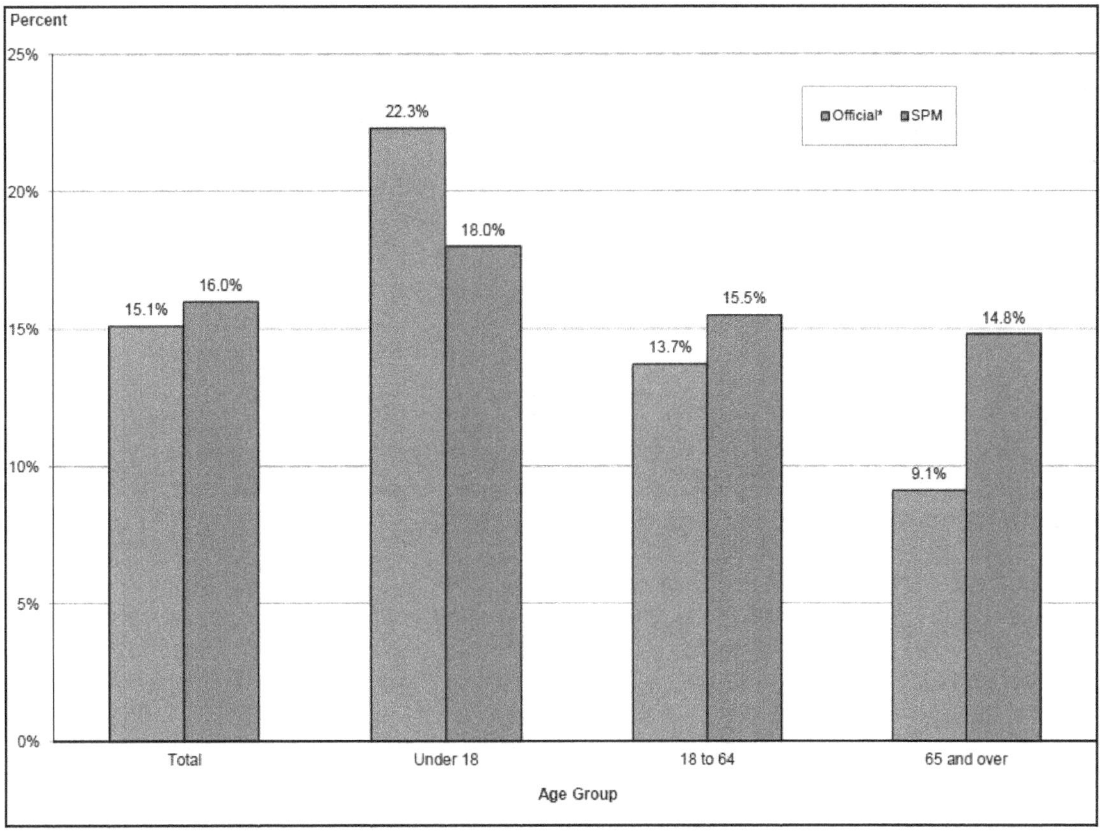

Source: Figure prepared by the Congressional Research Service (CRS), based on Kathleen Short, *The Research SUPPLEMENTAL POVERTY MEASURE: 2012*, U.S. Census Bureau, P60-247, Washington, DC, November 2013 http://www.census.gov/prod/2013pubs/p60-247.pdf.

* Differs from published "official" poverty rates as unrelated individuals under age 15 are included in the universe.

Poverty by Type of Economic Unit

As noted above, the SPM expands the definition of the economic unit considered for poverty measurement purposes over that used under the "official" poverty measure. The "official" poverty measure groups all co-residing household members related by marriage, birth, or adoption as sharing resources for purposes of poverty determination. Unrelated individuals, whether living alone as a single person household or with other unrelated members, are treated as separate economic units under the "official" poverty measure. The "official" measure also excludes unrelated children under age 15 from the universe for poverty determination. As noted earlier, the "adjusted official" poverty measure presented in this section of the report includes unrelated children, resulting in a 15.1% poverty rate as opposed to the published rate of 15.0% in 2012.

The SPM expands the economic unit used for poverty determination beyond that used by the "official" measure.[25] The SPM assesses the relationship of unrelated household members to others in the household to determine whether they will be joined with others to construct expanded economic units. For example, the SPM combines unrelated co-residing household members age 14 and older who are not married and who identify each other as boyfriend, girlfriend, or partner as cohabiting partners. Cohabiting partners, as well as any of their co-resident family members, are combined as an economic unit under the SPM. The SPM also combines unmarried co-residing parents of a child living in the household as an economic unit, even if the parents do not identify as a cohabiting couple. Any unrelated children who are under age 15 and are not foster children are assigned to the householder's economic unit, as are foster children under the age of 22. Additionally, the SPM combines children over age 18 living in a household with a parent, and any younger children of the parent, as an economic unit. Under the "official" poverty measure, a child age 18 and over is treated as an unrelated individual, and the child's parent is also treated as an unrelated individual if no other family members are present, or as an unrelated subfamily head if a spouse or other children (under age 18) are also residing in the household.

In 2012, an estimated 27.9 million persons, 9.0% of the 311.1 million persons represented in the CPS/ASEC, were classified as either joining an economic unit or having members added to their economic unit under the SPM measure, compared to how they would have been classified under the "official" measure's economic unit definition. Combining the resources of these additional household members had the effect of reducing poverty under the SPM measure, compared to the "official" measure, in 2012.

Figure 10 shows poverty rates in 2012 by type of economic unit. Persons identified as being in a married-couple unit, or in female- or male-householder units, are persons in those economic units whose members remained unchanged under the SPM compared to the "official" poverty measure. Persons who were added to an economic unit, or were part of an economic unit that had members added to it under the SPM definition, are labeled as being in a "new SPM unit." The figure shows that poverty rates for persons in married-couple units, and in male-householder units, are higher under the SPM than under the "official" poverty measure (10.0% versus 7.5% for persons in married-couple units, and 23.1% versus 17.9% for persons in male-householder units). Poverty rates for persons living in female-householder units did not statistically differ from one another, with about 3 out of 10 persons in such units considered poor under either measure. In contrast, poverty among persons who were members of "new SPM units" fell by over one-third, from 30.9% under the "official" measure to 18.4% under the SPM.

[25] For further discussion, see Ashley J. Provencher, *Unit of Analysis for Poverty Measurement: A Comparison of the Supplemental Poverty Measure and the Official Poverty Measure*, U.S. Census Bureau, SEHSD Working Paper # 2011-22, Washington, DC, August 2, 2011, http://www.census.gov/hhes/povmeas/methodology/supplemental/research/Provencher_JSM.pdf.

Figure 10. Poverty Rates Under the "Official"* and Research Supplemental Poverty Measures, by Type of Economic Unit: 2012

(Percent Poor)

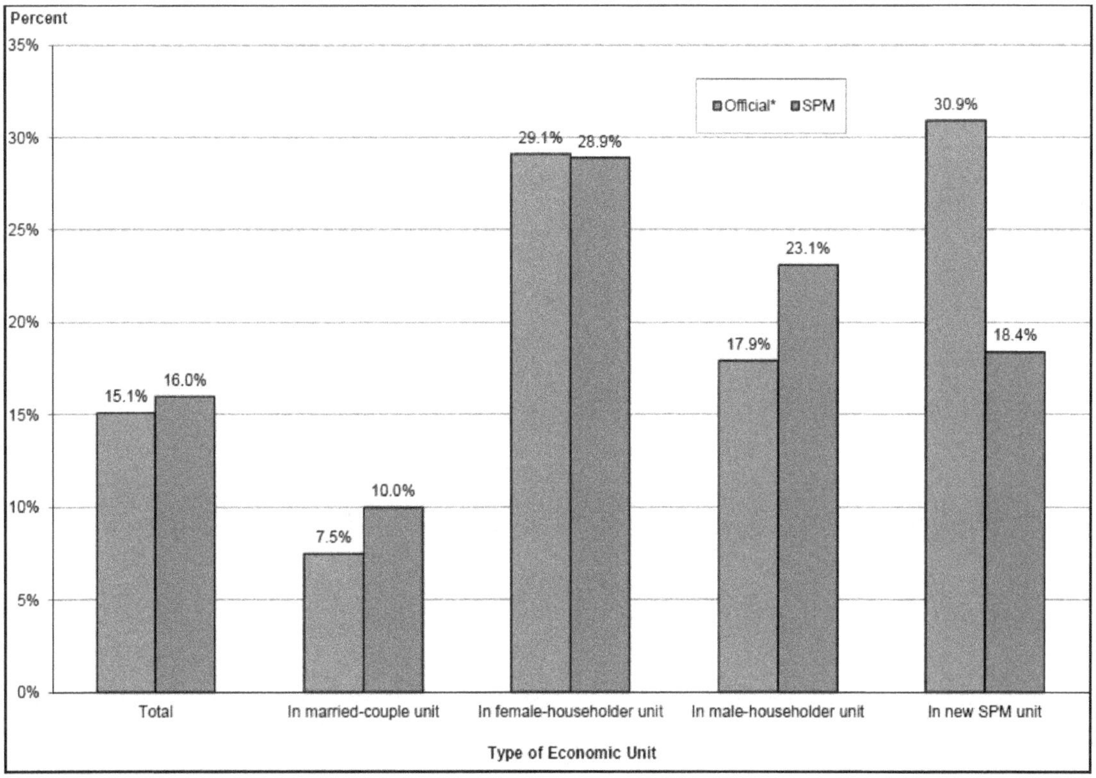

Source: Figure prepared by the Congressional Research Service (CRS), based on Kathleen Short, *The Research SUPPLEMENTAL POVERTY MEASURE: 2012*, U.S. Census Bureau, P60-247, Washington, DC, November 2013 http://www.census.gov/prod/2013pubs/p60-247.pdf.

* Differs from published "official" poverty rates as unrelated individuals under age 15 are included in the universe.

Poverty by Region

Figure 11 compares poverty rates in 2012 under the SPM with the "official" measure by Census region. The figure shows that poverty rates in the West are considerably higher (25% higher) under the SPM (19.0%) than under the "official" measure (15.2%). Poverty rates are about 13% higher in the Northeast under the SPM (15.5%) compared to the "official" measure (13.1%). Poverty rates in the Midwest are lower under the SPM than under the "official" measure, and in the South, essentially equal. The differences in poverty rates within and between regions based on the SPM compared to the "official" measure are most directly due to the SPM's geographic price adjustments to poverty thresholds for differences in the cost of housing in metropolitan and nonmetropolitan areas across states. The cost of housing tends to be higher in the West and Northeast, causing their poverty rates to rise under the SPM relative to the "official" measure and relative to the South and Midwest, where housing tends to be less expensive.

Figure 11. Poverty Rates Under the "Official"* and Research Supplemental Poverty Measures, by Region: 2012

(Percent Poor)

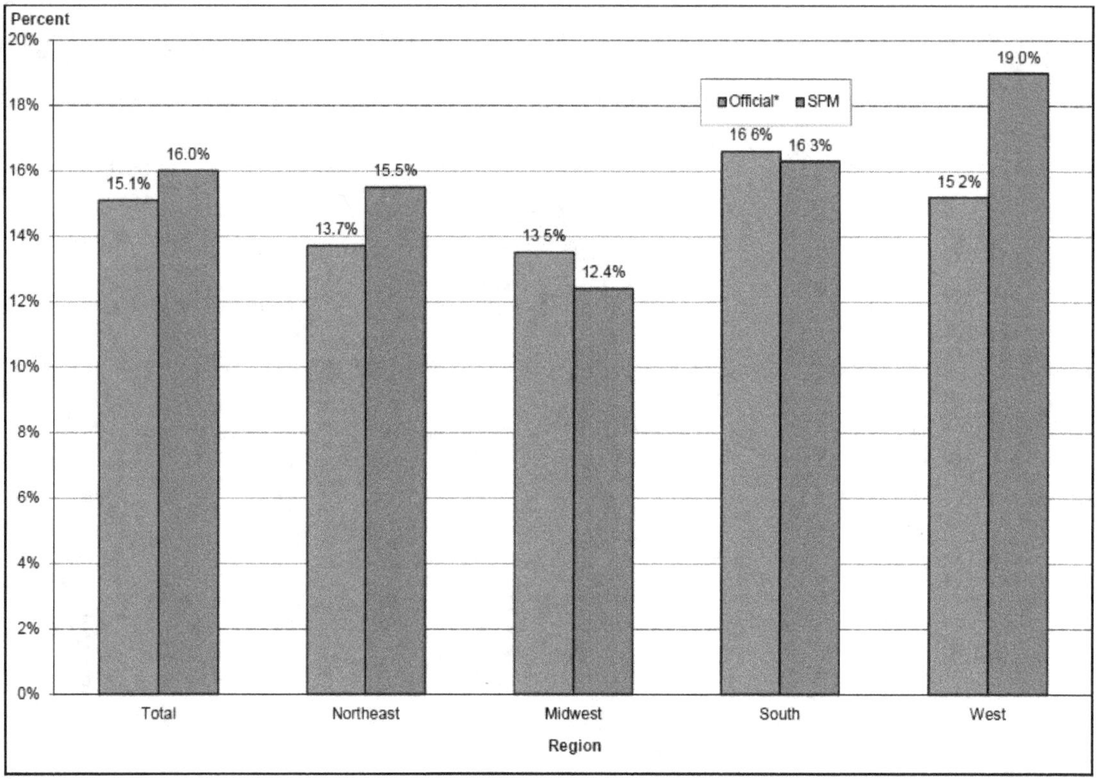

Source: Figure prepared by the Congressional Research Service (CRS), based on Kathleen Short, *The Research SUPPLEMENTAL POVERTY MEASURE: 2012*, U.S. Census Bureau, P60-247, Washington, DC, November 2013 http://www.census.gov/prod/2013pubs/p60-247.pdf.

* Differs from published "official" poverty rates as unrelated individuals under age 15 are included in the universe.

Poverty by Residence

Figure 12 depicts poverty rates by residence in metropolitan (principal city, and outside principal city [i.e., "suburban"]) and nonmetropolitan areas in 2012.[26] The figure shows that under the SPM, the poverty rate for persons living in Metropolitan Statistical Areas (MSAs) (16.4%) is somewhat higher than under the "official" measure (14.6%), whereas for persons living outside MSAs, the poverty rate is lower under the SPM (13.9%) than under the "official" measure (17.9%). Again, this most likely reflects differences in the cost of housing between MSAs and non-MSAs. Within MSAs, poverty rates are higher for persons living within principal cities under both measures than for people living outside them in "suburban" or "ex-urban" areas.

[26] The Census Bureau defines Metropolitan Statistical Areas (MSAs) containing a core urban area with a population of 50,000 or more, consisting of one or more counties, that includes the counties containing the urban core area as well as any adjacent counties that have a high degree of social and economic integration (as measured by commuting to work) with the urban core. See http://www.census.gov/population/metro/.

Figure 12. Poverty Rates Under the "Official"* and Research Supplemental Poverty Measures, by Residence: 2012

(Percent Poor)

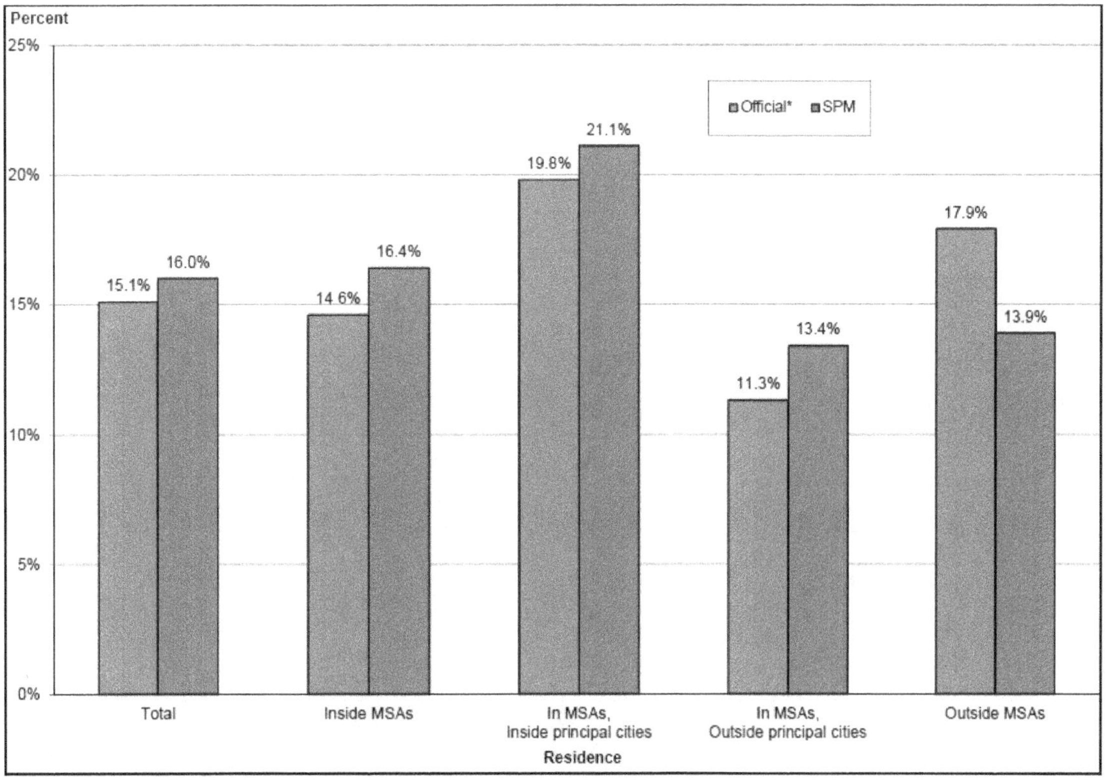

Source: Figure prepared by the Congressional Research Service (CRS), based on Kathleen Short, *The Research SUPPLEMENTAL POVERTY MEASURE: 2012*, U.S. Census Bureau, P60-247, Washington, DC, November 2013 http://www.census.gov/prod/2013pubs/p60-247.pdf.

* Differs from published "official" poverty rates as unrelated individuals under age 15 are included in the universe.

Poverty by State

Figure 13 depicts states according to whether the state's SPM poverty rate statistically differs from its "official" poverty rate.[27] Estimates are based on three-year (2010 to 2012) averages of CPS/ASEC data. Three years of data are combined in order to improve the statistical reliability of CPS/ASEC estimates at the state level. The figure shows that 13 states (California, Colorado, Connecticut, Florida, Hawaii, Illinois, Maryland, Massachusetts, New Hampshire, New Jersey, New York, Nevada, and Virginia) and the District of Columbia had higher poverty rates under the SPM than under the "official" measure. Among the 13 states with higher SPM poverty rates than their respective "official" poverty rate, only Colorado, Illinois, and Nevada were inland, and with the exception of Florida and Virginia, none were in the South. The figure shows that the SPM poverty rate was not statistically different than the "official" poverty rate in nine states (Alaska, Arizona, Delaware, Georgia, Oregon, Pennsylvania, Rhode Island, Utah, and Washington). Among the 28 remaining states in which their SPM poverty rates were lower than their respective

[27] Significant differences based on a 90% statistical confidence level.

"official" poverty rates, nearly all (with Maine being the exception) were either in the South, or inland.

Figure 13. Difference in Poverty Rates by State Using the "Official"* Measure and the SPM: Three-Year Average 2010-2012

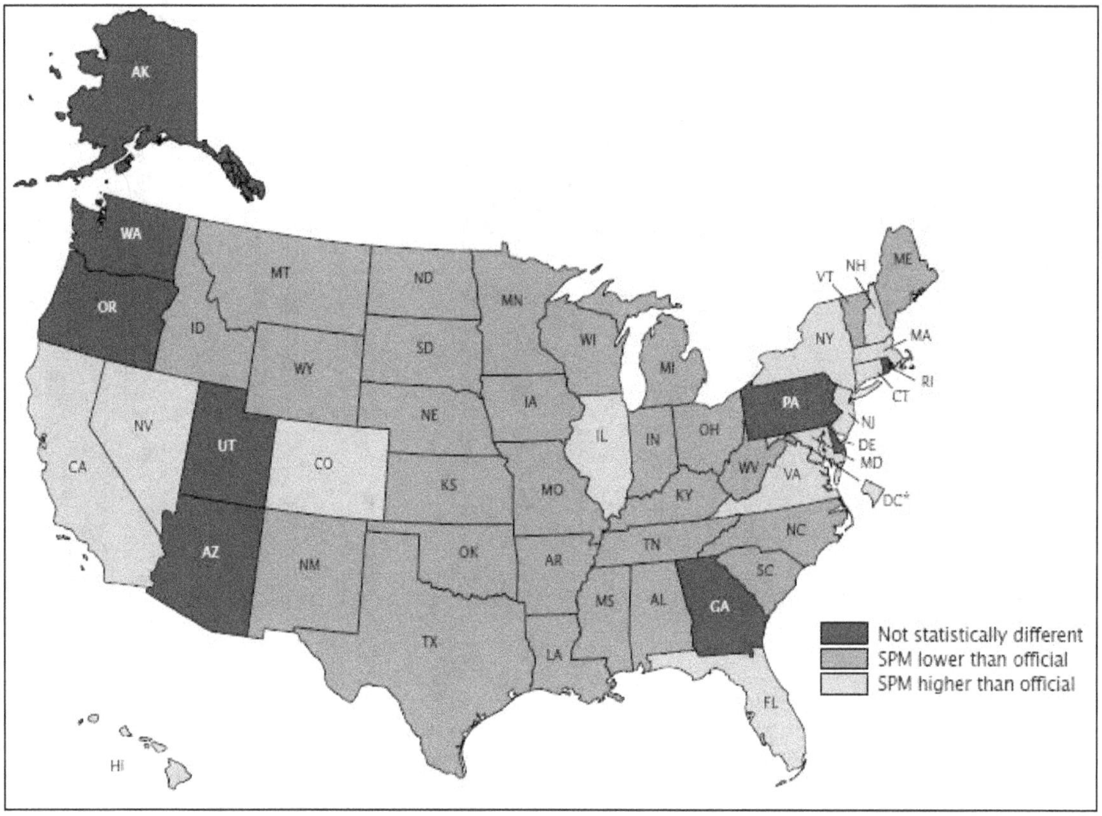

Source: Figure prepared by the Congressional Research Service (CRS), based on Kathleen Short, *The Research SUPPLEMENTAL POVERTY MEASURE: 2012*, U.S. Census Bureau, P60-247, Washington, DC, November 2013 http://www.census.gov/prod/2013pubs/p60-247.pdf.

Notes: Within state difference between official and SPM poverty rates determined at a 90% statistical confidence level.

* Differs from published "official" poverty rates as unrelated individuals under age 15 are included in the universe.

Figure 14 and **Figure 15** depict poverty rates by state under the official poverty measure and the SPM based on three years of CPS/ASEC data. Estimates are based on three-year (2010 to 2012) averages to improve the statistical reliability of estimates attainable from CPS/ASEC data at the state level. The two figures differ only in terms of the order in which states are sorted. In **Figure 14**, states are sorted from lowest to highest based on their respective "official" poverty rate point estimates, whereas in **Figure 15** states are sorted from lowest to highest based on their respective SPM poverty rate point estimates. In neither figure are precise rankings of states possible because of the depicted margin of error around each state's estimate. Within a state, a statistically significant difference[28] between a state's official poverty rate and its SPM poverty rate is signified

[28] Significant difference at a 90% statistical confidence level.

by solid-filled markers, indicating the point estimate under each measure, and a line connecting them, indicating the estimated difference (which is also shown in parentheses after each state name). The figures show the magnitude of the difference among the 13 states and the District of Columbia that had statistically significant higher poverty rates under the SPM than under the "official" measure, as well as for the 28 states in which the state's SPM rate was lower than its "official" poverty rate and the 9 states in which the incidence of poverty under the two measures did not differ statistically.

Differences in state poverty rates based on the SPM compared to the "official" measure may be due to a variety of factors. Geographic adjustments to SPM poverty income thresholds to account for differences in housing costs tend to result in higher poverty rates in areas with higher-priced housing than in areas with lower-priced housing. The mix of housing tenure (e.g., owner occupied, with or without a mortgage, renter occupied) may account for some of the difference between "official" and SPM poverty rates, within and between areas. Similarly, taxes may differ among areas. Also, populations may differ across areas in terms of household composition (e.g., share of households with cohabiting partners). The composition of the population based on age, or health insurance status, may also affect the incidence of SPM poverty relative to "official" poverty within and between geographic areas, by affecting medical out of pocket spending (MOOP), which is considered by SPM in estimating poverty.

Among the states with a statistically significant *increase* in poverty under the SPM, California's poverty rate increased by more than any other state's, increasing from 16.5% under the "official" measure to 23.8% under the SPM, or 7.3 percentage points. Under the "official" measure, California's poverty rate was substantially above the U.S. rate (15.1%), but under the SPM, California's poverty rate is estimated as the highest in the nation.

Other states with comparatively large increases in their poverty rates (in the four percentage point range) under the SPM compared to the "official" measure include Hawaii (an increase from 12.0% to 17.3%), Florida (a 15.5% to 19.5% increase), and New Jersey (a 10.7% to 15.5% increase).

Three states had decreases in their SPM poverty rate compared to their "official" rate in the four percentage point range. Mississippi and New Mexico, among the states with the highest "official" poverty (20.7% and 20.3%, respectively), both have an estimated SPM poverty rate of 16.1%—just about equal to the U.S. SPM rate (16.0%). West Virginia's "official" poverty rate (17.2%) is well above the "official" U.S. rate (15.1%), but its SPM rate (12.9%) falls well below the U.S. SPM rate (16.0%).

Figure 14. Poverty Rates by State Using the "Official"* Measure and the SPM: Three-Year Average 2010-2012

(States Ranked in Ascending Order by Official Poverty Rate; Percentage Point Difference in Parentheses)

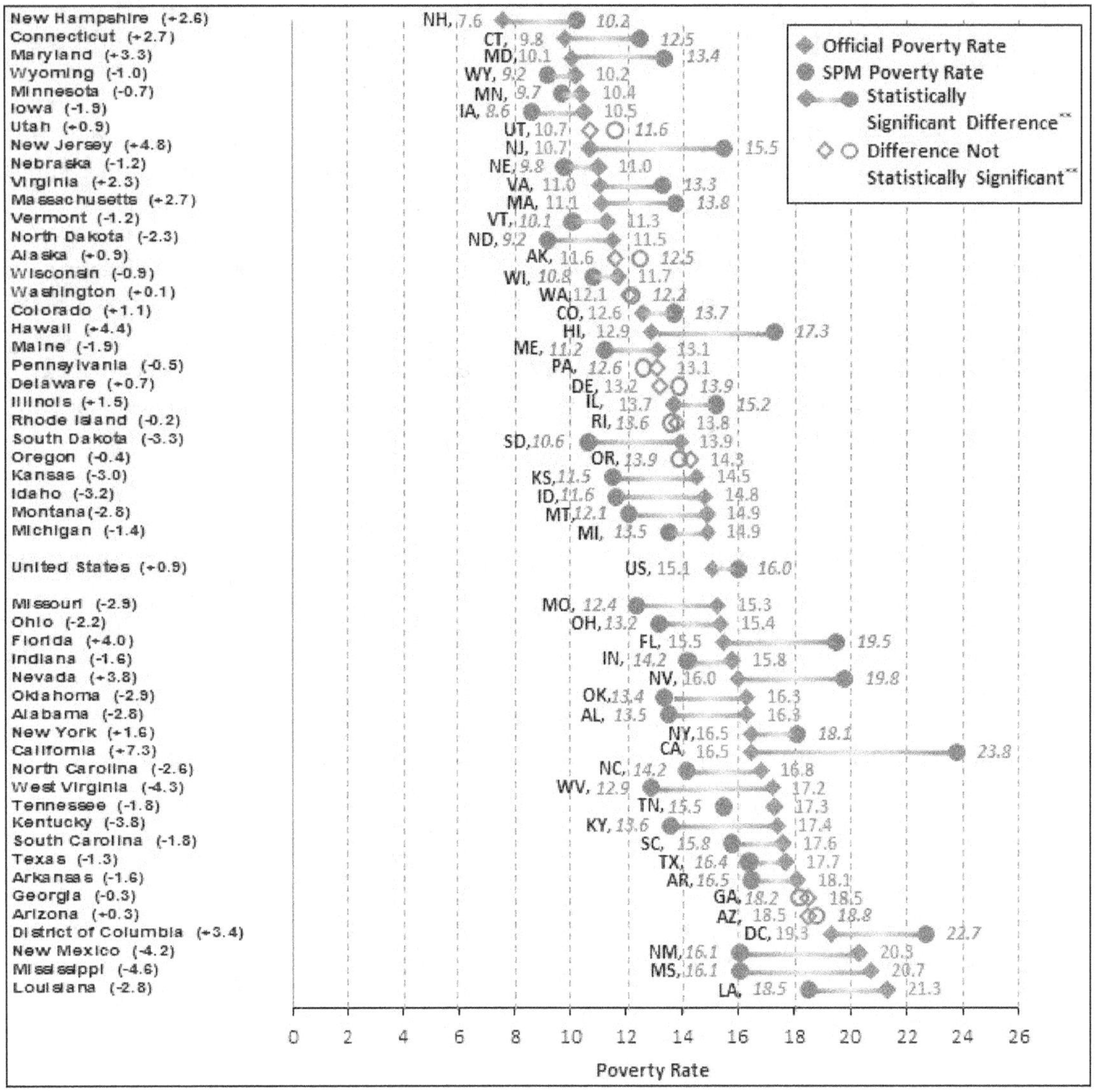

Source: Figure prepared by the Congressional Research Service (CRS), based on Kathleen Short, *The Research SUPPLEMENTAL POVERTY MEASURE: 2012*, U.S. Census Bureau, P60-247, Washington, DC, November 2013 http://www.census.gov/prod/2013pubs/p60-247.pdf.

* Differs from published "official" poverty rates as unrelated individuals under age 15 are included in the universe.

** Within state difference between official and SPM poverty rates determined at a 90% statistical confidence level.

Figure 15. Poverty Rates by State Using the "Official"* Measure and the SPM: Three-Year Average 2010-2012

(States Ranked in Ascending Order by SPM Poverty Rate; Percentage Point Difference in Parentheses)

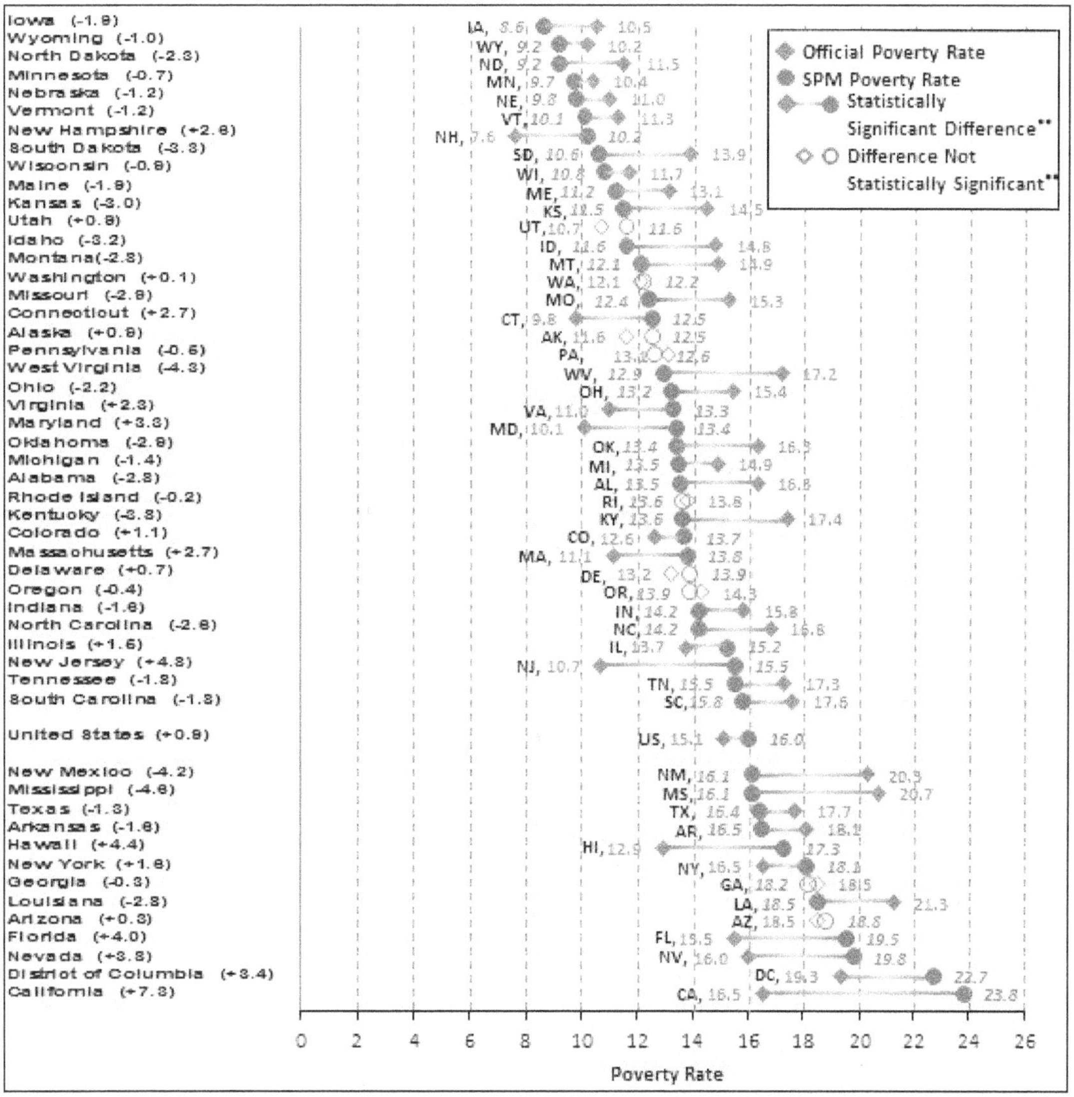

Source: Figure prepared by the Congressional Research Service (CRS), based on Kathleen Short, *The Research SUPPLEMENTAL POVERTY MEASURE: 2012*, U.S. Census Bureau, P60-247, Washington, DC, November 2013 http://www.census.gov/prod/2013pubs/p60-247.pdf

* Differs from published "official" poverty rates as unrelated individuals under age 15 are included in the universe.

** Within state difference between official and SPM poverty rates determined at a 90% statistical confidence level.

Marginal Effects of Counting Specified Resources and Expenses on Poverty Under the SPM

Figure 16 focuses strictly on the SPM, examining the marginal effects on poverty rates attributable to the inclusion of each selected income/resource or expenditure element on the measure. The marginal effects of each element on the SPM are displayed by age group. Elements that marginally contribute resources, and thereby have a poverty reducing effect when included in the SPM, are ranked from left to right in terms of their effect on poverty reduction among all persons. Similarly, expenditure elements, which are subtracted from resources and thereby marginally increase poverty as measured by the SPM, are ranked from left to right by their marginal poverty increasing effects on all persons.

The figure shows, for example, that the EITC has a greater poverty reducing effect than any of the other depicted resource elements. Overall, the EITC lowers the SPM poverty rate for all persons by 3.0 percentage points. The EITC is followed by SNAP benefits (1.6 percentage point reduction), housing subsidies (0.9 percentage point reduction), school lunch (0.4 percentage point reduction), and WIC and LIHEAP (each with a 0.1 percentage point reduction).

In contrast, on the expenditure side, child support paid to members outside the household has a relatively small effect on increasing the overall poverty rate. Federal income taxes before considering refundable credits, such as the EITC (counted on the resource side), result in an increase in overall poverty of 0.4 percentage points. FICA payroll taxes have a larger effect on marginal poverty (1.6 percentage point increase) than federal income taxes, as do work expenses (1.9 percentage points). Among all of the expense elements presented, medical out of pocket expenses (MOOP) contribute to the largest increase in poverty (3.4 percentage point increase for all persons).

Among the three age groups, the additional resources included in the SPM have a greater effect on reducing poverty among children (persons under age 18) and poverty among working age adults (ages 18 to 64) than on the aged (age 65 and older), with the exception of housing subsidies, which reduce the aged poverty rate by about the same amount as that of children. The EITC has a greater effect of reducing poverty among children (6.7 percentage point reduction) than any of the other added SPM resources.

On the expenditure side, FICA payroll taxes and work expenses have a greater effect on increasing poverty among children (due to a working parent) and non-aged adults than on the aged, who are less likely to be in the labor force and incur work-related taxes and expenses. Notably, under the SPM, MOOP expenses contribute to a substantial increase in poverty among the aged, contributing to a 6.4 percentage point increase in their poverty rate.

The relative distribution of additional resources and expenses in the SPM by age group helps to explain why poverty among children is lower under the SPM than it is under the "official" measure, whereas it is considerably higher for the aged.

Figure 16. Percentage Point Change in Poverty Rates Attributable to Selected Income and Expenditure Elements Under the Research Supplemental Poverty Measure, by Age Group: 2012

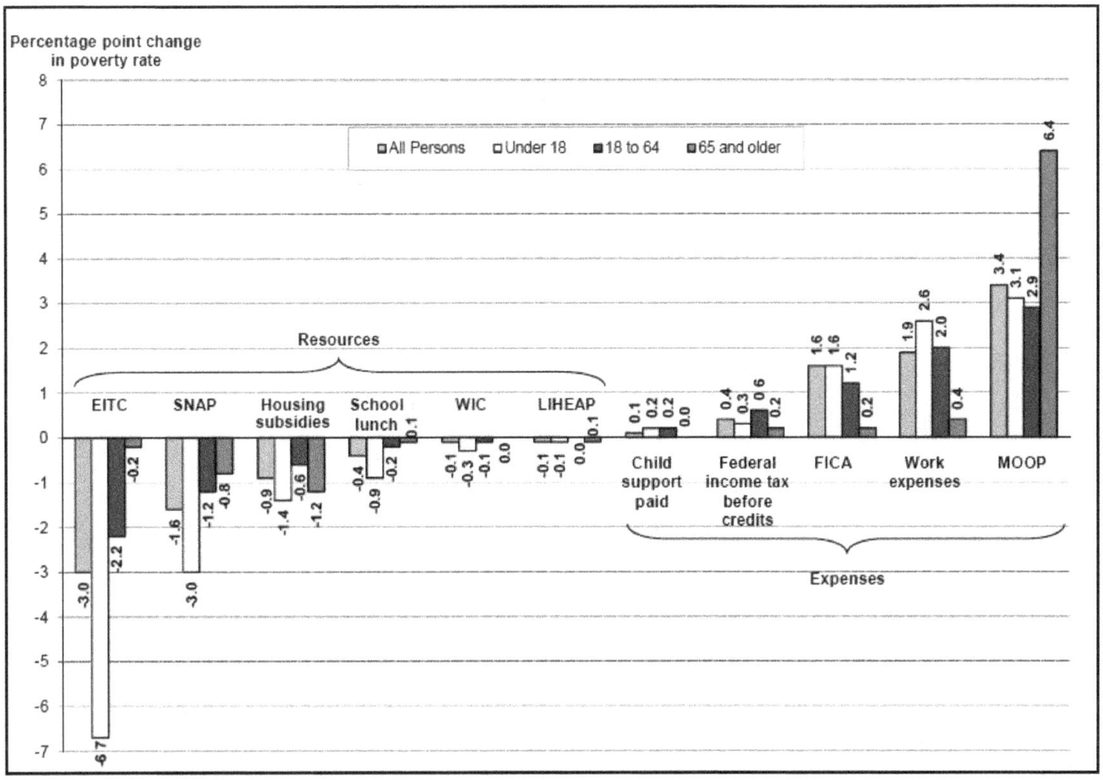

Source: Figure prepared by the Congressional Research Service (CRS), based on Kathleen Short, *The Research SUPPLEMENTAL POVERTY MEASURE: 2012*, U.S. Census Bureau, P60-247, Washington, DC, November 2013 http://www.census.gov/prod/2013pubs/p60-247.pdf.

Distribution of the Population by Ratio of Income/Resources Relative to Poverty

Figure 17 shows the distribution of the population by age group according to the degree to which their income and resources fall below or above poverty under the "official" and SPM definitions. The figure breaks out the poor population, depicted by brackets, into the share whose income and resources fall below half of their respective poverty lines (a classification sometimes referred to as "deep poverty") and the remainder. Others are categorized by the extent to which their income/resources exceed poverty under the two definitions, with those who fall below twice the poverty line also demarcated by brackets.

The figure shows, for example, that the share of children in "deep poverty" under the SPM is considerably lower than under the "official" measure (4.7% compared to 10.3%). As shown earlier, the SPM child poverty rate (18.0%) is lower than the "official" rate (22.3%). However, under the SPM, a much greater share of children live in "families" with income/resources between one and two times the poverty line than under the "official" measure (33.7% and 21.9%). Altogether, well over half of the children live in "families" having income/resources below twice the poverty line under the SPM (55.7%) compared to over two-fifths (44.2%) under the "official" measure. Thus, while the SPM appears to result in fewer children being counted as poor than under the "official" measure, under the SPM a greater share than under the "official" measure are concentrated at income levels just above poverty.

Among persons age 65 and over, a greater share are poor under the SPM than under the "official" measure, as shown earlier (14.8% compared to 9.1%), and a greater share are in "deep poverty" under the SPM (4.7%) than under the "official" measure (2.7%). In contrast to the "official" measure, under which about one-third (32.3%) of the aged have income below 200% of poverty, almost half (47.1%) have income/resources below that level under the SPM.

Figure 17. Distribution of the Population by Income/Resources to Poverty Ratios Under the "Official"* and Research Supplemental Poverty Measures, by Age Group: 2012

(Percent distribution)

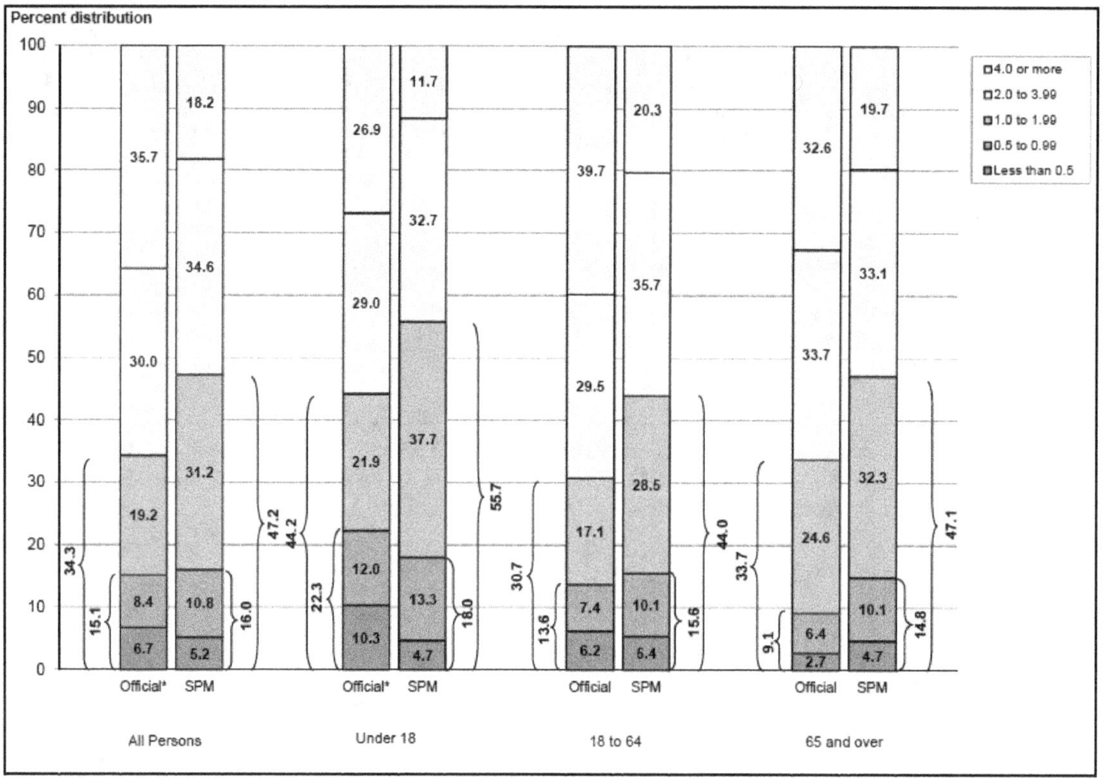

Source: Figure prepared by the Congressional Research Service (CRS), based on Kathleen Short, *The Research SUPPLEMENTAL POVERTY MEASURE: 2012*, U.S. Census Bureau, P60-247, Washington, DC, November 2013 http://www.census.gov/prod/2013pubs/p60-247.pdf.

* Differs from published "official" poverty rates as unrelated individuals under age 15 are included in the universe.

Discussion

As a research measure, the SPM offers potential for improved insight leading to better understanding of the nature and circumstances of those deemed to be among the nation's most economically and socially vulnerable. The SPM offers the means to better assess the performance of the economy, government policies, and programs with regard to the population's ability to secure sufficient income/resources to be able to meet basic expenditures for food, clothing, shelter, and utilities (plus "a little bit more").

The SPM counts considerably more elderly as poor than does the "official" measure. Medical expenses appear to be the driving factor in increasing poverty among the elderly under the SPM (see **Figure 16**). While not negating the improvement in the poverty status of the aged over the years, based on the "official" measure (see **Figure 2**), the SPM points more directly to the economic vulnerability of the aged, based not on income/resources alone, but rather, medical expenses competing for income that might otherwise be used to meet basic needs (i.e., FCSU plus "a little bit more"). Rising medical costs in society overall and individuals' personal health and insurance statuses pose potential economic risk to the aged being able to meet basic needs, as captured by FCSU-based poverty thresholds. The SPM provides additional insight that poverty reduction among the elderly depends not only on improving income, but also on their ability to reduce exposure to high medical expenses through "affordable" insurance. Rising medical costs in society also place the aged at increased risk of poverty under the SPM. It is worth noting that the SPM does not consider financial assets, other than interest, dividends, and annuity income from those assets, nor non-liquid assets (e.g., home equity) in determining poverty status. The SPM therefore does not address the means or extent to which the aged might tap those assets to meet medical or other needs.

The SPM results in fewer children being counted as poor than under the "official" measure. Still, the incidence of child poverty under the SPM, as under the "official" measure, exceeds that of the aged, but by a much slimmer margin (see **Figure 9**). Work-based supports, which both encourage work and help to offset the costs of going to work, appear be especially important to families with children, as captured by the SPM. The EITC, not counted under the "official" measure, significantly reduces child poverty as measured by the SPM, helping to offset taxes and work-related expenses working families with children incur (also captured by the SPM, but not under the "official" measure) (see **Figure 16**). The lack of safe, reliable, and affordable child care may limit parents' attachment to the labor force, contributing to poverty by reducing earnings that parents might otherwise secure. The SPM recognizes child care as a necessary expense many families face in their decisions relating to work by subtracting work-related child care expenses from income/resources that might otherwise go to meeting basic needs (i.e., FCSU plus "a little bit more"). As a consequence, the SPM should be sensitive to measuring the effects of child care programs and policies on child care affordability and poverty. The SPM captures the policy effects of assisting the poor through the provision of in-kind benefits, as opposed to just cash, whereas the "official" measure does not. For example, SNAP benefits, not captured under the "official" poverty measure, appear to have a sizeable effect in reducing child poverty under the SPM. Additionally, the expansion of the economic unit under the SPM to include cohabiting partners and their relatives may also contribute to lower child poverty rates under the SPM than under the "official" poverty measure, which is based on family ties defined by blood, marriage, and adoption.

Appendix A. U.S. Poverty Statistics: 1959-2012

Table A-1. Poverty Rates (Percent Poor) for Selected Groups, 1959-2012

		Related Children Under Age18[a]			Adults		Race/Ethnicity[b]—All Ages				
Year	All Persons	Total	In Female-Headed Families	In All Other Families	Ages 18-64	Age 65+	White[b]	White Non-Hispanic[b]	Black[b]	Hispanic	Asian[b]
2012	15.0	21.3	47.2	12.5	13.7	9.1	12.7b	9.7b	27.2b	25.6	11.7b
2011	15.0	21.4	47.6	12.1	13.7	8.7	12.8b	9.8b	27.6b	25.3	12.3b
2010r	15.1	21.5	46.6	12.9	13.8	8.9	13.0b	9.9b	27.4b	26.5	12.2b
2009	14.3	20.1	44.4	12.3	12.9	8.9	12.3b	9.4b	25.8b	25.3	12.5b
2008	13.2	18.5	43.5	10.7	11.7	9.7	11.2b	8.6b	24.7b	23.2	11.8b
2007	12.5	17.6	43.0	9.5	10.9	9.7	10.5b	8.2b	24.5b	21.5	10.2b
2006	12.3	16.9	42.1	9.0	10.8	9.4	10.3b	8.2b	24.3b	20.6	10.3b
2005	12.6	17.1	42.8	9.3	11.1	10.1	10.6b	8.3b	24.9b	21.8	11.1b
2004r	12.7	17.3	41.9	9.7	11.3	9.8	10.8b	8.7b	24.7b	21.9	9.8b
2003	12.5	17.2	41.8	9.6	10.8	10.2	10.5b	8.2b	24.4b	22.5	11.8b
2002	12.1	16.3	39.6	9.2	10.6	10.4	10.2b	8.0b	24.1b	21.8	10.1b
2001	11.7	15.8	39.3	8.8	10.1	10.1	9.9	7.8	22.7	21.4	n/a
2000r	11.3	15.6	40.1	8.6	9.6	9.9	9.5	7.4	22.5	21.5	n/a
1999	11.8	16.3	41.9	9.0	10.0	9.7	9.8	7.7	23.6	22.8	n/a
1998	12.7	18.3	46.1	9.7	10.5	10.5	10.5	8.2	26.1	25.6	n/a
1997	13.3	19.2	49.0	10.2	10.9	10.5	11.0	8.6	26.5	27.1	n/a
1996	13.7	19.8	49.3	10.9	11.3	10.8	11.2	8.6	28.4	29.4	n/a
1995	13.8	20.2	50.3	10.7	11.4	10.5	11.2	8.5	29.3	30.3	n/a
1994	14.5	21.2	52.9	11.7	11.9	11.7	11.7	9.4	30.6	30.7	n/a
1993	15.1	22.0	53.7	12.4	12.4	12.2	12.2	9.9	33.1	30.6	n/a
1992r	14.8	21.6	54.6	11.8	11.9	12.9	11.9	9.6	33.4	29.6	n/a
1991r	14.2	21.1	55.5	11.1	11.4	12.4	11.3	9.4	32.7	28.7	n/a
1990	13.5	19.9	53.4	10.7	10.7	12.2	10.7	8.8	31.9	28.1	n/a
1989	12.8	19.0	51.1	10.4	10.2	11.4	10.0	8.3	30.7	26.2	n/a
1988r	13.0	19.0	52.9	10.0	10.5	12.0	10.1	8.4	31.3	26.7	n/a
1987r	13.4	19.7	54.7	10.9	10.6	12.5	10.4	8.7	32.4	28.0	n/a
1986	13.6	19.8	54.4	10.8	10.8	12.4	11.0	9.4	31.1	27.3	n/a
1985	14.0	20.1	53.6	11.7	11.3	12.6	11.4	9.7	31.3	29.0	n/a
1984	14.4	21.0	54.0	12.5	11.7	12.4	11.5	10.0	33.8	28.4	n/a
1983	15.2	21.8	55.5	13.5	12.4	13.8	12.2	10.8	35.7	28.1	n/a

Year	All Persons	Related Children Under Age18[a] Total	In Female-Headed Families	In All Other Families	Adults Ages 18-64	Age 65+	Race/Ethnicity[b]—All Ages White[b]	White Non-Hispanic[b]	Black[b]	Hispanic	Asian[b]
1982	15.0	21.3	56.0	13.0	12.0	14.6	12.0	10.6	35.6	29.9	n/a
1981	14.0	19.5	52.3	11.6	11.1	15.3	11.1	9.9	34.2	26.5	n/a
1980	13.0	17.9	50.8	10.4	10.1	15.7	10.2	9.1	32.5	25.7	n/a
1979	11.7	16.0	48.6	8.5	8.9	15.2	9.0	8.1	31.0	21.8	n/a
1978	11.4	15.7	50.6	7.9	8.7	14.0	8.7	7.9	30.6	21.6	n/a
1977	11.6	16.0	50.3	8.5	8.8	14.1	8.9	8.0	31.3	22.4	n/a
1976	11.8	15.8	52.0	8.5	9.0	15.0	9.1	8.1	31.1	24.7	n/a
1975	12.3	16.8	52.7	9.8	9.2	15.3	9.7	8.6	31.3	26.9	n/a
1974	11.2	15.1	51.5	8.3	8.3	14.6	8.6	7.7	30.3	23.0	n/a
1973	11.1	14.2	52.1	7.6	8.3	16.3	8.4	7.5	31.4	21.9	n/a
1972	11.9	14.9	53.1	8.6	8.8	18.6	9.0	n/a	33.3	n/a	n/a
1971	12.5	15.1	53.1	9.3	9.3	21.6	9.9	n/a	32.5	n/a	n/a
1970	12.6	14.9	53.0	9.2	9.0	24.6	9.9	n/a	33.5	n/a	n/a
1969	12.1	13.8	54.4	8.6	8.7	25.3	9.5	n/a	32.2	n/a	n/a
1968	12.8	15.3	55.2	10.2	9.0	25.0	10.0	n/a	34.7	n/a	n/a
1967	14.2	16.3	54.3	11.5	10.0	29.5	11.0	n/a	39.3	n/a	n/a
1966	14.7	17.4	58.2	12.6	10.5	28.5	11.3	n/a	41.8	n/a	n/a
1959	22.4	26.9	72.2	22.4	17.0	35.2	18.1	n/a	55.1	n/a	n/a

Source: Prepared by the Congressional Research Service using U.S. Bureau of the Census data based on the "official" measure of poverty.

Notes: r = revised estimates. n/a = not available.

a. Beginning in 1979, restricted to children in primary families only. Before 1979, includes children in unrelated subfamilies.

b. Beginning in 2002, CPS respondents could identify themselves as being of more than one race. Consequently, racial data for 2002 and after are not comparable to earlier years. Here, in 2002 and after, the term white means of white race alone, the term black means of black race alone, and the term Asian means Asian alone. Hispanics, who may be of any race, are included among whites and blacks unless otherwise noted.

Appendix B. Metropolitan Area Poverty Estimates

Table B-1. Metropolitan Area Poverty: 2012

		Number Poor		Poverty Rate (Percent Poor)				
Metropolitan Area	Total Population	Estimate	Margin of Error[a]	Poverty Rate	Margin of Error[a]	Difference 2011 vs. 2010 Poverty Rate[b]		Rank[c]
Abilene, TX	156,020	31,991	+/-4,101	20.5%	+/-2.6%	3.6%	▲	61
Akron, OH	687,031	107,952	+/-7,892	15.7%	+/-1.1%	-0.9%		205
Albany, GA	148,869	40,011	+/-4,170	26.9%	+/-2.8%	-1.5%		8
Albany-Schenectady-Troy, NY	843,802	93,228	+/-6,350	11.0%	+/-0.8%	-0.4%		335
Albuquerque, NM	887,938	164,484	+/-9,170	18.5%	+/-1.0%	-1.9%	▼	107
Alexandria, LA	146,869	32,184	+/-4,402	21.9%	+/-3.0%	-1.3%		42
Allentown-Bethlehem-Easton, PA-NJ	804,602	84,127	+/-6,553	10.5%	+/-0.8%	-1.4%	▼	346
Altoona, PA	124,522	15,955	+/-2,286	12.8%	+/-1.8%	-1.5%		297
Amarillo, TX	245,710	43,548	+/-5,530	17.7%	+/-2.2%	2.2%		133
Ames, IA	82,352	17,880	+/-2,472	21.7%	+/-3.0%	-2.3%		44
Anchorage, AK	384,749	33,353	+/-4,104	8.7%	+/-1.1%	-0.1%		361
Anderson, IN	123,288	18,763	+/-2,891	15.2%	+/-2.3%	-4.3%	▼	224
Anderson, SC	186,924	33,612	+/-4,647	18.0%	+/-2.5%	3.2%		124
Ann Arbor, MI	334,662	55,178	+/-5,538	16.5%	+/-1.6%	-0.5%		171
Anniston-Oxford, AL	114,001	25,270	+/-3,403	22.2%	+/-3.0%	1.0%		38
Appleton, WI	225,045	18,885	+/-2,630	8.4%	+/-1.2%	1.0%		362
Asheville, NC	422,827	66,980	+/-5,197	15.8%	+/-1.2%	-1.1%		201
Athens-Clarke County, GA	183,413	44,991	+/-3,612	24.5%	+/-1.9%	-5.4%	▼	16
Atlanta-Sandy Springs-Marietta, GA	5,352,236	887,901	+/-29,846	16.6%	+/-0.6%	-0.2%		166

		Number Poor		Poverty Rate (Percent Poor)			
Metropolitan Area	Total Population	Estimate	Margin of Error[a]	Poverty Rate	Margin of Error[a]	Difference 2011 vs. 2010 Poverty Rate[b]	Rank[c]
Atlantic City-Hammonton, NJ	269,061	39,381	+/-5,807	14.6%	+/-2.2%	1.2%	246
Auburn-Opelika, AL	141,938	34,970	+/-3,720	24.6%	+/-2.6%	1.7%	15
Augusta-Richmond County, GA-SC	553,981	112,218	+/-8,963	20.3%	+/-1.6%	1.3%	66
Austin-Round Rock-San Marcos, TX	1,795,080	278,461	+/-16,086	15.5%	+/-0.9%	0.3%	211
Bakersfield-Delano, CA	825,020	196,625	+/-13,837	23.8%	+/-1.7%	-0.7%	23
Baltimore-Towson, MD	2,685,159	303,704	+/-14,893	11.3%	+/-0.6%	-0.3%	329
Bangor, ME	146,973	26,664	+/-3,346	18.1%	+/-2.3%	0.6%	118
Barnstable Town, MA	212,878	21,947	+/-3,653	10.3%	+/-1.7%	1.1%	350
Baton Rouge, LA	791,990	148,176	+/-10,354	18.7%	+/-1.3%	1.1%	103
Battle Creek, MI	131,723	23,569	+/-3,069	17.9%	+/-2.3%	-1.7%	129
Bay City, MI	105,729	13,622	+/-2,199	12.9%	+/-2.1%	0.4%	293
Beaumont-Port Arthur, TX	371,641	71,066	+/-6,392	19.1%	+/-1.7%	1.6%	95
Bellingham, WA	199,626	33,039	+/-4,080	16.6%	+/-2.0%	0.9%	169
Bend, OR	161,035	27,003	+/-5,184	16.8%	+/-3.2%	3.5%	163
Billings, MT	157,398	19,325	+/-2,698	12.3%	+/-1.7%	-0.5%	307
Binghamton, NY	238,176	36,879	+/-3,933	15.5%	+/-1.6%	-0.6%	213
Birmingham-Hoover, AL	1,114,744	186,891	+/-11,466	16.8%	+/-1.0%	0.2%	164
Bismarck, ND	110,290	7,266	+/-1,572	6.6%	+/-1.4%	-2.2%	365
Blacksburg-Christiansburg-Radford, VA	152,492	36,188	+/-3,820	23.7%	+/-2.4%	2.4%	24
Bloomington, IN	180,522	41,518	+/-4,489	23.0%	+/-2.5%	1.2%	30
Bloomington-Normal, IL	163,412	25,664	+/-2,990	15.7%	+/-1.8%	-0.2%	206
Boise City-Nampa, ID	624,906	96,368	+/-10,276	15.4%	+/-1.6%	-0.8%	217
Boston-Cambridge-Quincy, MA-NH	4,486,468	479,126	+/-15,238	10.7%	+/-0.3%	0.0%	343

Metropolitan Area	Total Population	Number Poor: Estimate	Number Poor: Margin of Error[a]	Poverty Rate (Percent Poor): Poverty Rate	Margin of Error[a]	Difference 2011 vs. 2010 Poverty Rate[b]	Rank[c]
Boulder, CO	295,728	42,978	+/-4,392	14.5%	+/-1.5%	0.5%	252
Bowling Green, KY	121,147	23,918	+/-3,162	19.7%	+/-2.6%	1.3%	86
Bremerton-Silverdale, WA	246,659	27,164	+/-4,015	11.0%	+/-1.6%	0.3%	336
Bridgeport-Stamford-Norwalk, CT	915,813	81,629	+/-7,143	8.9%	+/-0.8%	-0.5%	358
Brownsville-Harlingen, TX	411,003	148,267	+/-9,666	36.1%	+/-2.3%	2.0%	1
Brunswick, GA	108,902	20,221	+/-3,440	18.6%	+/-3.1%	0.1%	105
Buffalo-Niagara Falls, NY	1,104,704	157,407	+/-8,287	14.2%	+/-0.7%	-0.5%	263
Burlington, NC	150,197	30,525	+/-3,985	20.3%	+/-2.7%	1.8%	64
Burlington-South Burlington, VT	202,994	22,433	+/-2,554	11.1%	+/-1.3%	0.0%	334
Canton-Massillon, OH	393,938	57,474	+/-4,951	14.6%	+/-1.3%	-1.9%	250
Cape Coral-Fort Myers, FL	636,067	97,210	+/-7,188	15.3%	+/-1.1%	-0.1%	221
Cape Girardeau-Jackson, MO-IL	92,459	16,386	+/-2,696	17.7%	+/-2.9%	-0.7%	134
Carson City, NV	52,680	8,987	+/-2,353	17.1%	+/-4.5%	3.6%	153
Casper, WY	76,446	9,816	+/-1,839	12.8%	+/-2.4%	1.7%	295
Cedar Rapids, IA	254,225	24,150	+/-3,246	9.5%	+/-1.3%	-0.9%	355
Champaign-Urbana, IL	217,140	42,982	+/-4,172	19.8%	+/-1.9%	-3.0% ▼	84
Charleston, WV	300,542	45,089	+/-4,874	15.0%	+/-1.6%	-3.2% ▼	236
Charleston-North Charleston-Summerville, SC	679,648	103,056	+/-7,728	15.2%	+/-1.1%	-1.8%	225
Charlotte-Gastonia-Rock Hill, NC-SC	1,801,914	272,027	+/-12,223	15.1%	+/-0.7%	-0.6%	231
Charlottesville, VA	193,616	26,922	+/-4,417	13.9%	+/-2.3%	0.9%	269
Chattanooga, TN-GA	524,863	83,083	+/-7,256	15.8%	+/-1.4%	-1.8%	202
Cheyenne, WY	91,949	9,822	+/-2,954	10.7%	+/-3.2%	1.6%	342
Chicago-Joliet-Naperville, IL-IN-WI	9,372,358	1,362,635	+/-30,184	14.5%	+/-0.3%	-0.2%	251

Metropolitan Area	Total Population	Number Poor		Poverty Rate (Percent Poor)			
		Estimate	Margin of Error[a]	Poverty Rate	Margin of Error[a]	Difference 2011 vs. 2010 Poverty Rate[b]	Rank[c]
Chico, CA	216,391	47,693	+/-5,041	22.0%	+/-2.3%	-1.0%	40
Cincinnati-Middletown, OH-KY-IN	2,100,460	313,902	+/-13,545	14.9%	+/-0.6%	0.7%	238
Clarksville, TN-KY	277,225	53,501	+/-6,208	19.3%	+/-2.2%	0.9%	94
Cleveland, TN	115,747	22,933	+/-4,094	19.8%	+/-3.5%	-1.2%	83
Cleveland-Elyria-Mentor, OH	2,021,864	314,832	+/-11,325	15.6%	+/-0.6%	-0.4%	208
Coeur d'Alene, ID	140,564	16,630	+/-3,373	11.8%	+/-2.4%	-4.8% ▼	320
College Station-Bryan, TX	219,226	57,006	+/-5,130	26.0%	+/-2.3%	-3.9% ▼	9
Colorado Springs, CO	649,651	83,308	+/-8,024	12.8%	+/-1.2%	-0.1%	296
Columbia, MO	167,502	32,391	+/-3,877	19.3%	+/-2.3%	-1.5%	93
Columbia, SC	751,020	122,507	+/-9,448	16.3%	+/-1.3%	-1.3%	184
Columbus, GA-AL	291,315	54,555	+/-5,654	18.7%	+/-1.9%	1.6%	102
Columbus, IN	77,948	10,107	+/-3,297	13.0%	+/-4.2%	-0.5%	291
Columbus, OH	1,828,401	275,385	+/-14,679	15.1%	+/-0.8%	-0.3%	233
Corpus Christi, TX	428,154	69,385	+/-6,938	16.2%	+/-1.6%	-3.8% ▼	188
Corvallis, OR	81,776	18,961	+/-3,400	23.2%	+/-4.1%	-2.2%	27
Crestview-Fort Walton Beach-Destin, FL	184,163	25,349	+/-4,122	13.8%	+/-2.2%	-1.1%	276
Cumberland, MD-WV	93,858	15,330	+/-2,516	16.3%	+/-2.7%	-2.9%	181
Dallas-Fort Worth-Arlington, TX	6,561,480	984,719	+/-23,684	15.0%	+/-0.4%	-0.8% ▼	235
Dalton, GA	141,605	30,654	+/-4,636	21.6%	+/-3.3%	1.7%	46
Danville, IL	77,863	14,165	+/-2,986	18.2%	+/-3.8%	-1.5%	116
Danville, VA	103,108	18,218	+/-2,893	17.7%	+/-2.8%	-1.4%	138
Davenport-Moline-Rock Island, IA-IL	372,959	43,774	+/-3,939	11.7%	+/-1.1%	-0.9%	321
Dayton, OH	815,446	137,732	+/-10,406	16.9%	+/-1.3%	-0.7%	158

		Number Poor		Poverty Rate (Percent Poor)			
Metropolitan Area	Total Population	Estimate	Margin of Error[a]	Poverty Rate	Margin of Error[a]	Difference 2011 vs. 2010 Poverty Rate[b]	Rank[c]
Decatur, AL	152,271	26,929	+/-4,140	17.7%	+/-2.7%	0.7%	137
Decatur, IL	106,872	24,953	+/-2,901	23.3%	+/-2.7%	9.5% ▲	26
Deltona-Daytona Beach-Ormond Beach, FL	486,465	96,125	+/-7,463	19.8%	+/-1.5%	2.6% ▲	85
Denver-Aurora-Broomfield, CO	2,608,939	332,043	+/-15,260	12.7%	+/-0.6%	-0.1%	299
Des Moines-West Des Moines, IA	577,570	70,870	+/-7,393	12.3%	+/-1.3%	1.1%	308
Detroit-Warren-Livonia, MI	4,248,945	740,712	+/-20,248	17.4%	+/-0.5%	-0.6%	144
Dothan, AL	145,259	28,928	+/-2,460	19.9%	+/-1.7%	1.2%	79
Dover, DE	162,155	19,330	+/-3,763	11.9%	+/-2.3%	-2.5%	312
Dubuque, IA	91,565	11,447	+/-2,024	12.5%	+/-2.2%	3.3% ▲	305
Duluth, MN-WI	268,927	41,082	+/-3,386	15.3%	+/-1.3%	-1.4%	222
Durham-Chapel Hill, NC	498,686	89,222	+/-7,518	17.9%	+/-1.5%	-0.5%	130
Eau Claire, WI	155,515	21,478	+/-2,737	13.8%	+/-1.8%	1.4%	272
El Centro, CA	164,473	37,332	+/-5,169	22.7%	+/-3.1%	-4.1%	31
El Paso, TX	812,645	195,247	+/-10,809	24.0%	+/-1.3%	-0.6%	21
Elizabethtown, KY	116,810	17,635	+/-3,210	15.1%	+/-2.7%	-0.5%	230
Elkhart-Goshen, IN	195,801	30,249	+/-4,738	15.4%	+/-2.4%	-5.1% ▼	215
Elmira, NY	83,915	12,243	+/-2,120	14.6%	+/-2.5%	-1.4%	249
Erie, PA	267,909	42,462	+/-3,860	15.8%	+/-1.4%	-0.6%	200
Eugene-Springfield, OR	347,917	78,203	+/-6,911	22.5%	+/-2.0%	1.1%	34
Evansville, IN-KY	347,895	48,616	+/-5,690	14.0%	+/-1.6%	-0.3%	268
Fairbanks, AK	96,529	6,646	+/-1,813	6.9%	+/-1.9%	-3.5%	364
Fargo, ND-MN	208,133	22,118	+/-2,954	10.6%	+/-1.4%	-3.5% ▼	344
Farmington, NM	126,992	26,324	+/-3,243	20.7%	+/-2.6%	3.6%	59

Metropolitan Area	Total Population	Number Poor		Poverty Rate (Percent Poor)			
		Estimate	Margin of Error[a]	Poverty Rate	Margin of Error[a]	Difference 2011 vs. 2010 Poverty Rate[b]	Rank[c]
Fayetteville, NC	362,499	61,869	+/-5,946	17.1%	+/-1.6%	-1.5%	152
Fayetteville-Springdale-Rogers, AR-MO	470,725	82,980	+/-8,224	17.6%	+/-1.7%	0.4%	139
Flagstaff, AZ	127,795	33,191	+/-4,344	26.0%	+/-3.4%	4.1%	10
Flint, MI	412,418	88,137	+/-6,951	21.4%	+/-1.7%	0.8%	49
Florence, SC	201,858	43,134	+/-4,783	21.4%	+/-2.4%	-0.1%	50
Florence-Muscle Shoals, AL	144,910	27,196	+/-3,724	18.8%	+/-2.6%	2.3%	101
Fond du Lac, WI	98,703	8,608	+/-1,938	8.7%	+/-2.0%	-0.9%	360
Fort Collins-Loveland, CO	302,392	42,316	+/-4,411	14.0%	+/-1.5%	-0.2%	267
Fort Smith, AR-OK	292,035	66,011	+/-5,561	22.6%	+/-1.9%	2.1%	32
Fort Wayne, IN	414,634	62,557	+/-5,884	15.1%	+/-1.4%	-1.0%	232
Fresno, CA	930,872	264,738	+/-13,321	28.4%	+/-1.4%	2.7% ▲	5
Gadsden, AL	102,682	21,819	+/-3,915	21.2%	+/-3.8%	0.3%	52
Gainesville, FL	254,375	70,552	+/-5,754	27.7%	+/-2.2%	3.6% ▲	6
Gainesville, GA	182,805	37,000	+/-5,945	20.2%	+/-3.3%	2.8%	67
Glens Falls, NY	124,271	14,242	+/-2,612	11.5%	+/-2.1%	-3.1%	328
Goldsboro, NC	121,372	30,174	+/-4,262	24.9%	+/-3.5%	1.5%	14
Grand Forks, ND-MN	93,134	16,629	+/-2,265	17.9%	+/-2.4%	3.0%	132
Grand Junction, CO	144,569	23,285	+/-4,260	16.1%	+/-2.9%	4.8% ▲	192
Grand Rapids-Wyoming, MI	770,026	126,882	+/-9,164	16.5%	+/-1.2%	1.8% ▲	173
Great Falls, MT	79,862	15,919	+/-2,657	19.9%	+/-3.3%	4.3%	76
Greeley, CO	255,850	37,734	+/-5,186	14.7%	+/-2.0%	0.0%	242
Green Bay, WI	303,843	34,897	+/-3,993	11.5%	+/-1.3%	1.2%	327
Greensboro-High Point, NC	718,572	130,400	+/-8,783	18.1%	+/-1.2%	0.5%	117

Metropolitan Area	Total Population	Number Poor: Estimate	Number Poor: Margin of Error[a]	Poverty Rate (Percent Poor): Poverty Rate	Poverty Rate (Percent Poor): Margin of Error[a]	Poverty Rate (Percent Poor): Difference 2011 vs. 2010 Poverty Rate[b]		Rank[c]
Greenville, NC	185,538	45,060	+/-4,358	24.3%	+/-2.3%	-1.1%		19
Greenville-Mauldin-Easley, SC	630,562	111,529	+/-8,864	17.7%	+/-1.4%	0.2%		136
Gulfport-Biloxi, MS	250,861	50,407	+/-6,494	20.1%	+/-2.6%	-1.7%		69
Hagerstown-Martinsburg, MD-WV	263,149	38,424	+/-6,225	14.6%	+/-2.4%	1.0%		247
Hanford-Corcoran, CA	131,214	27,819	+/-4,294	21.2%	+/-3.3%	0.7%		53
Harrisburg-Carlisle, PA	536,028	66,476	+/-6,615	12.4%	+/-1.2%	1.9%	▲	306
Harrisonburg, VA	119,527	26,436	+/-3,424	22.1%	+/-2.9%	6.4%	▲	39
Hartford-West Hartford-East Hartford, CT	1,169,356	127,371	+/-7,291	10.9%	+/-0.6%	-0.5%		338
Hattiesburg, MS	143,389	36,577	+/-4,869	25.5%	+/-3.4%	1.2%		12
Hickory-Lenoir-Morganton, NC	355,419	71,802	+/-6,072	20.2%	+/-1.7%	1.8%		68
Hinesville-Fort Stewart, GA	81,660	13,250	+/-2,842	16.2%	+/-3.4%	-2.7%		187
Holland-Grand Haven, MI	259,849	29,263	+/-4,634	11.3%	+/-1.8%	-0.8%		330
Honolulu, HI	945,975	97,754	+/-8,616	10.3%	+/-0.9%	0.2%		349
Hot Springs, AR	95,147	18,951	+/-3,488	19.9%	+/-3.7%	-1.9%		78
Houma-Bayou Cane-Thibodaux, LA	205,153	32,847	+/-4,949	16.0%	+/-2.4%	-2.9%		194
Houston-Sugar Land-Baytown, TX	6,123,358	1,005,192	+/-32,475	16.4%	+/-0.5%	-1.0%	▼	176
Huntington-Ashland, WV-KY-OH	277,846	50,941	+/-4,448	18.3%	+/-1.6%	-1.5%		112
Huntsville, AL	419,921	50,052	+/-6,323	11.9%	+/-1.5%	-2.1%		313
Idaho Falls, ID	132,174	18,157	+/-3,400	13.7%	+/-2.6%	0.0%		277
Indianapolis-Carmel, IN	1,764,733	253,758	+/-13,144	14.4%	+/-0.7%	0.3%		256
Iowa City, IA	149,364	22,596	+/-2,802	15.1%	+/-1.9%	-3.6%	▼	226
Ithaca, NY	89,419	16,194	+/-2,444	18.1%	+/-2.7%	-2.9%		119
Jackson, MI	150,510	29,934	+/-3,371	19.9%	+/-2.2%	4.6%	▲	81

Metropolitan Area	Total Population	Number Poor		Poverty Rate (Percent Poor)			
		Estimate	Margin of Error[a]	Poverty Rate	Margin of Error[a]	Difference 2011 vs. 2010 Poverty Rate[b]	Rank[c]
Jackson, MS	531,354	117,984	+/-8,520	22.2%	+/-1.6%	3.7% ▲	36
Jackson, TN	110,454	19,155	+/-3,275	17.3%	+/-2.9%	-3.3%	146
Jacksonville, FL	1,349,273	211,746	+/-12,970	15.7%	+/-1.0%	0.5%	207
Jacksonville, NC	169,165	20,586	+/-4,627	12.2%	+/-2.7%	-3.1%	309
Janesville, WI	156,384	24,314	+/-3,399	15.5%	+/-2.2%	0.5%	210
Jefferson City, MO	139,737	21,555	+/-4,364	15.4%	+/-3.1%	3.1%	216
Johnson City, TN	194,031	37,682	+/-4,368	19.4%	+/-2.2%	-0.3%	91
Johnstown, PA	133,355	19,334	+/-1,996	14.5%	+/-1.5%	0.5%	253
Jonesboro, AR	118,862	23,465	+/-2,594	19.7%	+/-2.2%	-2.8%	87
Joplin, MO	170,601	30,537	+/-3,179	17.9%	+/-1.9%	2.4%	128
Kalamazoo-Portage, MI	321,649	58,206	+/-5,144	18.1%	+/-1.6%	-2.7% ▼	120
Kankakee-Bradley, IL	108,498	19,501	+/-3,052	18.0%	+/-2.8%	1.3%	125
Kansas City, MO-KS	2,028,356	261,177	+/-12,866	12.9%	+/-0.6%	-0.6%	294
Kennewick-Pasco-Richland, WA	263,116	38,061	+/-5,468	14.5%	+/-2.1%	-2.2%	254
Killeen-Temple-Fort Hood, TX	396,374	59,346	+/-7,124	15.0%	+/-1.8%	-0.6%	237
Kingsport-Bristol-Bristol, TN-VA	303,555	49,814	+/-4,486	16.4%	+/-1.5%	0.3%	177
Kingston, NY	174,348	23,289	+/-3,333	13.4%	+/-1.9%	-1.3%	284
Knoxville, TN	692,519	114,308	+/-8,259	16.5%	+/-1.2%	2.3% ▲	170
Kokomo, IN	96,226	16,312	+/-2,692	17.0%	+/-2.8%	0.2%	155
La Crosse, WI-MN	130,138	18,643	+/-2,428	14.3%	+/-1.9%	-0.4%	259
Lafayette, IN	192,060	37,781	+/-4,160	19.7%	+/-2.2%	-1.4%	89
Lafayette, LA	274,176	48,959	+/-5,542	17.9%	+/-2.0%	-0.7%	131
Lake Charles, LA	196,595	32,376	+/-5,320	16.5%	+/-2.7%	-2.1%	175

Metropolitan Area	Total Population	Number Poor: Estimate	Number Poor: Margin of Error[a]	Poverty Rate (Percent Poor): Poverty Rate	Poverty Rate (Percent Poor): Margin of Error[a]	Poverty Rate (Percent Poor): Difference 2011 vs. 2010 Poverty Rate[b]	Rank[c]
Lake Havasu City-Kingman, AZ	188,318	40,839	+/-5,092	21.7%	+/-2.7%	0.0%	45
Lakeland-Winter Haven, FL	600,528	107,634	+/-9,321	17.9%	+/-1.5%	-1.5%	127
Lancaster, PA	512,363	60,668	+/-6,325	11.8%	+/-1.2%	0.9%	317
Lansing-East Lansing, MI	444,349	88,802	+/-6,259	20.0%	+/-1.4%	1.4%	73
Laredo, TX	254,758	81,651	+/-7,394	32.1%	+/-2.9%	-0.8%	3
Las Cruces, NM	209,622	56,903	+/-6,722	27.1%	+/-3.2%	-3.6%	7
Las Vegas-Paradise, NV	1,975,043	323,075	+/-17,482	16.4%	+/-0.9%	-0.5%	179
Lawrence, KS	103,379	21,682	+/-3,136	21.0%	+/-3.0%	4.3% ▲	58
Lawton, OK	116,943	19,673	+/-3,289	16.8%	+/-2.8%	-0.2%	161
Lebanon, PA	132,340	17,214	+/-3,310	13.0%	+/-2.5%	1.9%	288
Lewiston, ID-WA	60,012	6,228	+/-1,172	10.4%	+/-1.9%	-2.6%	348
Lewiston-Auburn, ME	104,067	16,593	+/-3,308	15.9%	+/-3.2%	-0.5%	196
Lexington-Fayette, KY	465,971	73,317	+/-5,342	15.7%	+/-1.1%	-1.6%	204
Lima, OH	101,238	20,634	+/-2,501	20.4%	+/-2.5%	1.1%	63
Lincoln, NE	295,065	39,122	+/-4,057	13.3%	+/-1.4%	-1.6%	285
Little Rock-North Little Rock-Conway, AR	702,794	106,269	+/-9,483	15.1%	+/-1.3%	0.4%	227
Logan, UT-ID	124,385	20,341	+/-3,271	16.4%	+/-2.6%	-0.3%	180
Longview, TX	207,901	39,312	+/-5,783	18.9%	+/-2.8%	2.7%	99
Longview, WA	100,232	16,756	+/-2,587	16.7%	+/-2.6%	-3.8%	165
Los Angeles-Long Beach-Santa Ana, CA	12,862,222	2,266,193	+/-42,491	17.6%	+/-0.3%	0.6% ▲	140
Louisville/Jefferson County, KY-IN	1,276,908	205,800	+/-11,405	16.1%	+/-0.9%	0.8%	191
Lubbock, TX	280,353	63,145	+/-6,022	22.5%	+/-2.1%	1.6%	33
Lynchburg, VA	245,012	41,295	+/-4,526	16.9%	+/-1.8%	0.8%	159

		Number Poor		Poverty Rate (Percent Poor)			
Metropolitan Area	Total Population	Estimate	Margin of Error[a]	Poverty Rate	Margin of Error[a]	Difference 2011 vs. 2010 Poverty Rate[b]	Rank[c]
Macon, GA	223,684	51,844	+/-5,327	23.2%	+/-2.4%	0.4%	28
Madera-Chowchilla, CA	144,053	33,936	+/-5,216	23.6%	+/-3.6%	-0.7%	25
Madison, WI	568,248	72,210	+/-6,056	12.7%	+/-1.1%	0.1%	300
Manchester-Nashua, NH	394,445	38,552	+/-5,913	9.8%	+/-1.5%	1.5%	354
Manhattan, KS	126,071	18,782	+/-2,587	14.9%	+/-2.0%	-2.1%	240
Mankato-North Mankato, MN	91,630	14,261	+/-2,180	15.6%	+/-2.4%	-1.6%	209
Mansfield, OH	114,896	21,729	+/-3,694	18.9%	+/-3.2%	1.9%	98
McAllen-Edinburg-Mission, TX	796,479	274,713	+/-17,146	34.5%	+/-2.2%	-3.3% ▼	2
Medford, OR	204,278	36,200	+/-4,410	17.7%	+/-2.2%	-2.5%	135
Memphis, TN-MS-AR	1,307,830	259,780	+/-10,892	19.9%	+/-0.8%	0.6%	82
Merced, CA	256,771	62,448	+/-6,157	24.3%	+/-2.4%	-3.1%	18
Miami-Fort Lauderdale-Pompano Beach, FL	5,691,607	993,904	+/-25,832	17.5%	+/-0.5%	-0.3%	143
Michigan City-La Porte, IN	101,470	18,234	+/-3,042	18.0%	+/-3.0%	0.0%	126
Midland, TX	145,188	9,086	+/-2,649	6.3%	+/-1.8%	-5.5% ▼	366
Milwaukee-Waukesha-West Allis, WI	1,538,274	244,236	+/-10,721	15.9%	+/-0.7%	0.7%	198
Minneapolis-St. Paul-Bloomington, MN-WI	3,299,784	352,560	+/-14,086	10.7%	+/-0.4%	-0.4%	341
Missoula, MT	107,931	14,875	+/-2,691	13.8%	+/-2.5%	-3.6%	274
Mobile, AL	403,118	84,891	+/-7,046	21.1%	+/-1.7%	1.6%	54
Modesto, CA	515,955	104,559	+/-10,039	20.3%	+/-1.9%	-3.5% ▼	65
Monroe, LA	168,014	43,435	+/-5,407	25.9%	+/-3.2%	-2.0%	11
Monroe, MI	149,901	17,822	+/-3,208	11.9%	+/-2.1%	-0.3%	316
Montgomery, AL	365,843	65,904	+/-5,630	18.0%	+/-1.5%	-2.3%	122
Morgantown, WV	124,165	26,783	+/-3,774	21.6%	+/-3.0%	3.5%	47

Metropolitan Area	Total Population	Number Poor		Poverty Rate (Percent Poor)			
		Estimate	Margin of Error[a]	Poverty Rate	Margin of Error[a]	Difference 2011 vs. 2010 Poverty Rate[b]	Rank[c]
Morristown, TN	134,219	28,636	+/-4,274	21.3%	+/-3.2%	1.3%	51
Mount Vernon-Anacortes, WA	116,756	17,129	+/-3,180	14.7%	+/-2.7%	-0.5%	244
Muncie, IN	108,782	24,147	+/-2,799	22.2%	+/-2.5%	-0.8%	37
Muskegon-Norton Shores, MI	163,408	35,899	+/-3,251	22.0%	+/-2.0%	2.0%	41
Myrtle Beach-North Myrtle Beach-Conway, SC	279,367	55,937	+/-5,642	20.0%	+/-2.0%	1.2%	71
Napa, CA	135,439	11,996	+/-2,747	8.9%	+/-2.0%	-5.7% ▼	359
Naples-Marco Island, FL	328,790	45,297	+/-6,294	13.8%	+/-1.9%	-3.2% ▼	275
Nashville-Davidson—Murfreesboro—Franklin, TN	1,608,546	229,686	+/-11,403	14.3%	+/-0.7%	-0.4%	262
New Haven-Milford, CT	838,123	113,308	+/-9,061	13.5%	+/-1.1%	0.3%	280
New Orleans-Metairie-Kenner, LA	1,185,940	230,153	+/-12,716	19.4%	+/-1.1%	-0.1%	92
New York-Northern New Jersey-Long Island, NY-NJ-PA	18,842,228	2,785,196	+/-40,070	14.8%	+/-0.2%	0.4% ▲	241
Niles-Benton Harbor, MI	151,403	31,081	+/-3,413	20.5%	+/-2.2%	3.5% ▲	60
North Port-Bradenton-Sarasota, FL	710,287	98,127	+/-8,323	13.8%	+/-1.2%	0.4%	271
Norwich-New London, CT	262,896	24,105	+/-3,537	9.2%	+/-1.3%	0.4%	356
Ocala, FL	326,435	59,762	+/-6,936	18.3%	+/-2.1%	1.2%	113
Ocean City, NJ	93,825	8,392	+/-2,201	8.9%	+/-2.3%	-2.4%	357
Odessa, TX	142,261	17,866	+/-3,799	12.6%	+/-2.7%	-1.4%	304
Ogden-Clearfield, UT	556,266	56,638	+/-7,028	10.2%	+/-1.3%	0.1%	352
Oklahoma City, OK	1,266,689	204,759	+/-8,652	16.2%	+/-0.7%	-0.4%	190
Olympia, WA	255,368	32,269	+/-5,460	12.6%	+/-2.1%	-0.4%	302
Omaha-Council Bluffs, NE-IA	867,442	112,533	+/-7,709	13.0%	+/-0.9%	0.3%	290
Orlando-Kissimmee-Sanford, FL	2,184,723	369,925	+/-18,528	16.9%	+/-0.8%	1.0%	156
Oshkosh-Neenah, WI	158,389	17,772	+/-3,003	11.2%	+/-1.9%	-2.1%	331

Metropolitan Area	Total Population	Number Poor		Poverty Rate (Percent Poor)			
		Estimate	Margin of Error[a]	Poverty Rate	Margin of Error[a]	Difference 2011 vs. 2010 Poverty Rate[b]	Rank[c]
Owensboro, KY	114,458	19,260	+/-2,882	16.8%	+/-2.5%	1.4%	160
Oxnard-Thousand Oaks-Ventura, CA	824,845	94,910	+/-8,051	11.5%	+/-1.0%	0.3%	326
Palm Bay-Melbourne-Titusville, FL	540,315	79,606	+/-7,462	14.7%	+/-1.4%	0.7%	243
Palm Coast, FL	97,650	18,105	+/-4,402	18.5%	+/-4.5%	-0.5%	106
Panama City-Lynn Haven-Panama City Beach, FL	168,972	27,335	+/-3,863	16.2%	+/-2.3%	3.6%	189
Parkersburg-Marietta-Vienna, WV-OH	158,978	27,078	+/-3,745	17.0%	+/-2.3%	0.5%	154
Pascagoula, MS	161,607	27,744	+/-5,015	17.2%	+/-3.1%	-0.2%	151
Pensacola-Ferry Pass-Brent, FL	436,684	66,789	+/-7,128	15.3%	+/-1.6%	-0.1%	220
Peoria, IL	371,694	51,431	+/-4,800	13.8%	+/-1.3%	-1.1%	270
Philadelphia-Camden-Wilmington, PA-NJ-DE-MD	5,872,433	787,217	+/-20,430	13.4%	+/-0.3%	-0.1%	282
Phoenix-Mesa-Glendale, AZ	4,256,978	741,322	+/-19,794	17.4%	+/-0.5%	0.1%	145
Pine Bluff, AR	87,796	21,394	+/-2,992	24.4%	+/-3.4%	2.1%	17
Pittsburgh, PA	2,300,959	279,386	+/-12,179	12.1%	+/-0.5%	-0.5%	310
Pittsfield, MA	124,178	17,437	+/-2,447	14.0%	+/-2.0%	0.7%	265
Pocatello, ID	88,548	13,734	+/-2,142	15.5%	+/-2.4%	-3.1%	212
Port St. Lucie, FL	426,978	70,337	+/-7,757	16.5%	+/-1.8%	-1.8%	174
Portland-South Portland-Biddeford, ME	506,847	58,872	+/-5,826	11.6%	+/-1.1%	0.1%	324
Portland-Vancouver-Hillsboro, OR-WA	2,257,880	316,515	+/-12,596	14.0%	+/-0.6%	-1.0% ▼	266
Poughkeepsie-Newburgh-Middletown, NY	643,519	71,386	+/-5,981	11.1%	+/-0.9%	-1.1%	333
Prescott, AZ	210,176	30,085	+/-5,607	14.3%	+/-2.7%	-4.7% ▼	260
Providence-New Bedford-Fall River, RI-MA	1,544,740	209,423	+/-10,189	13.6%	+/-0.7%	-0.2%	279
Provo-Orem, UT	537,006	77,026	+/-8,274	14.3%	+/-1.5%	0.2%	257
Pueblo, CO	156,967	31,445	+/-5,020	20.0%	+/-3.2%	1.4%	70

Metropolitan Area	Total Population	Number Poor: Estimate	Number Poor: Margin of Error[a]	Poverty Rate (Percent Poor): Poverty Rate	Margin of Error[a]	Difference 2011 vs. 2010 Poverty Rate[b]	Rank[c]
Punta Gorda, FL	158,767	19,977	+/-3,576	12.6%	+/-2.3%	0.7%	303
Racine, WI	190,124	25,180	+/-3,648	13.2%	+/-1.9%	0.6%	286
Raleigh-Cary, NC	1,161,708	147,281	+/-12,117	12.7%	+/-1.0%	0.4%	301
Rapid City, SD	127,702	14,306	+/-2,631	11.2%	+/-2.1%	-1.6%	332
Reading, PA	400,861	58,702	+/-5,194	14.6%	+/-1.3%	0.9%	245
Redding, CA	175,830	29,131	+/-4,288	16.6%	+/-2.4%	-3.5%	168
Reno-Sparks, NV	428,289	78,085	+/-7,350	18.2%	+/-1.7%	5.2% ▲	114
Richmond, VA	1,241,253	147,786	+/-10,798	11.9%	+/-0.9%	-0.5%	314
Riverside-San Bernardino-Ontario, CA	4,269,169	813,251	+/-22,351	19.0%	+/-0.5%	1.1% ▲	96
Roanoke, VA	301,201	40,557	+/-5,319	13.5%	+/-1.8%	1.0%	281
Rochester, MN	185,704	18,663	+/-2,731	10.0%	+/-1.5%	2.8% ▲	353
Rochester, NY	1,017,927	146,943	+/-7,553	14.4%	+/-0.7%	-1.1%	255
Rockford, IL	340,208	51,876	+/-5,534	15.2%	+/-1.6%	-3.0% ▼	223
Rocky Mount, NC	147,370	35,431	+/-4,414	24.0%	+/-3.0%	2.3%	20
Rome, GA	92,236	22,067	+/-3,478	23.9%	+/-3.8%	4.3%	22
Sacramento—Arden-Arcade—Roseville, CA	2,164,537	366,076	+/-16,655	16.9%	+/-0.8%	0.8%	157
Saginaw-Saginaw Township North, MI	191,832	36,311	+/-4,179	18.9%	+/-2.2%	-0.5%	97
Salem, OR	387,397	77,184	+/-7,952	19.9%	+/-2.1%	0.4%	77
Salinas, CA	407,594	74,981	+/-7,735	18.4%	+/-1.9%	1.0%	108
Salisbury, MD	114,402	20,986	+/-3,855	18.3%	+/-3.3%	-0.9%	111
Salt Lake City, UT	1,146,949	146,232	+/-11,394	12.7%	+/-1.0%	-1.2%	298
San Angelo, TX	108,960	17,531	+/-3,452	16.1%	+/-3.1%	-1.5%	193
San Antonio-New Braunfels, TX	2,191,061	378,226	+/-16,970	17.3%	+/-0.8%	0.7%	148

Metropolitan Area	Total Population	Number Poor		Poverty Rate (Percent Poor)			Rank[c]
		Estimate	Margin of Error[a]	Poverty Rate	Margin of Error[a]	Difference 2011 vs. 2010 Poverty Rate[b]	
San Diego-Carlsbad-San Marcos, CA	3,098,088	465,295	+/-20,161	15.0%	+/-0.7%	-0.1%	234
San Francisco-Oakland-Fremont, CA	4,390,239	522,229	+/-18,993	11.9%	+/-0.4%	0.0%	315
San Jose-Sunnyvale-Santa Clara, CA	1,868,187	202,357	+/-12,662	10.8%	+/-0.7%	0.2%	339
San Luis Obispo-Paso Robles, CA	258,424	35,434	+/-4,476	13.7%	+/-1.7%	-1.5%	278
Sandusky, OH	75,482	7,849	+/-1,769	10.4%	+/-2.3%	-1.0%	347
Santa Barbara-Santa Maria-Goleta, CA	412,871	67,359	+/-6,548	16.3%	+/-1.6%	1.2%	183
Santa Cruz-Watsonville, CA	255,592	34,204	+/-5,394	13.4%	+/-2.1%	-1.4%	283
Santa Fe, NM	143,611	26,410	+/-3,893	18.4%	+/-2.7%	0.6%	109
Santa Rosa-Petaluma, CA	485,037	58,686	+/-7,459	12.1%	+/-1.5%	-0.1%	311
Savannah, GA	350,631	63,101	+/-7,239	18.0%	+/-2.1%	-1.0%	123
Scranton—Wilkes-Barre, PA	543,553	84,047	+/-5,818	15.5%	+/-1.1%	0.9%	214
Seattle-Tacoma-Bellevue, WA	3,495,234	409,239	+/-19,482	11.7%	+/-0.6%	-0.1%	322
Sebastian-Vero Beach, FL	138,273	23,747	+/-4,407	17.2%	+/-3.2%	3.7%	150
Sheboygan, WI	111,966	12,895	+/-2,804	11.5%	+/-2.5%	4.2% ▲	325
Sherman-Denison, TX	118,535	19,940	+/-3,613	16.8%	+/-3.0%	0.1%	162
Shreveport-Bossier City, LA	398,842	72,109	+/-6,763	18.1%	+/-1.7%	-0.8%	121
Sioux City, IA-NE-SD	140,363	22,280	+/-4,123	15.9%	+/-2.9%	1.5%	199
Sioux Falls, SD	232,585	23,762	+/-3,095	10.2%	+/-1.3%	0.9%	351
South Bend-Mishawaka, IN-MI	306,264	49,851	+/-4,717	16.3%	+/-1.5%	-1.7%	186
Spartanburg, SC	281,542	56,214	+/-6,233	20.0%	+/-2.2%	0.5%	75
Spokane, WA	460,580	73,314	+/-7,265	15.9%	+/-1.6%	1.0%	197
Springfield, IL	207,526	29,759	+/-3,814	14.3%	+/-1.8%	-2.4%	258
Springfield, MA	659,621	113,402	+/-7,393	17.2%	+/-1.1%	1.6%	149

Metropolitan Area	Total Population	Number Poor		Poverty Rate (Percent Poor)			
		Estimate	Margin of Error[a]	Poverty Rate	Margin of Error[a]	Difference 2011 vs. 2010 Poverty Rate[b]	Rank[c]
Springfield, MO	429,273	75,104	+/-6,517	17.5%	+/-1.5%	0.3%	142
Springfield, OH	134,297	27,462	+/-3,221	20.4%	+/-2.4%	0.9%	62
St. Cloud, MN	182,590	23,689	+/-3,121	13.0%	+/-1.7%	-1.0%	289
St. George, UT	141,984	23,127	+/-4,777	16.3%	+/-3.4%	0.7%	185
St. Joseph, MO-KS	119,694	19,727	+/-3,299	16.5%	+/-2.7%	1.3%	172
St. Louis, MO-IL	2,760,219	394,288	+/-15,820	14.3%	+/-0.6%	0.6%	261
State College, PA	138,830	29,123	+/-3,421	21.0%	+/-2.5%	0.3%	57
Steubenville-Weirton, OH-WV	118,196	18,878	+/-3,464	16.0%	+/-2.9%	-0.7%	195
Stockton, CA	688,873	126,610	+/-9,990	18.4%	+/-1.4%	0.3%	110
Sumter, SC	104,867	19,100	+/-4,094	18.2%	+/-3.9%	4.0%	115
Syracuse, NY	632,179	96,710	+/-5,663	15.3%	+/-0.9%	-0.9%	219
Tallahassee, FL	355,496	79,698	+/-6,974	22.4%	+/-2.0%	-0.4%	35
Tampa-St. Petersburg-Clearwater, FL	2,800,206	458,689	+/-17,744	16.4%	+/-0.6%	0.0%	178
Terre Haute, IN	160,903	31,421	+/-3,844	19.5%	+/-2.4%	2.5%	90
Texarkana, TX-Texarkana, AR	129,485	25,899	+/-3,579	20.0%	+/-2.7%	0.9%	72
Toledo, OH	630,598	125,508	+/-7,513	19.9%	+/-1.2%	-0.3%	80
Topeka, KS	229,172	34,186	+/-4,117	14.9%	+/-1.8%	2.3%	239
Trenton-Ewing, NJ	349,813	36,603	+/-4,606	10.5%	+/-1.3%	-1.0%	345
Tucson, AZ	968,447	193,466	+/-11,146	20.0%	+/-1.1%	-0.5%	74
Tulsa, OK	934,873	141,326	+/-6,152	15.1%	+/-0.7%	-0.2%	228
Tuscaloosa, AL	212,412	44,598	+/-4,731	21.0%	+/-2.2%	-1.0%	56
Tyler, TX	210,667	37,075	+/-5,207	17.6%	+/-2.5%	0.1%	141
Utica-Rome, NY	285,830	43,824	+/-3,549	15.3%	+/-1.2%	-1.8%	218

Metropolitan Area	Total Population	Number Poor		Poverty Rate (Percent Poor)			Rank[c]
		Estimate	Margin of Error[a]	Poverty Rate	Margin of Error[a]	Difference 2011 vs. 2010 Poverty Rate[b]	
Valdosta, GA	141,423	35,793	+/-4,891	25.3%	+/-3.4%	-2.3%	13
Vallejo-Fairfield, CA	407,797	59,515	+/-5,383	14.6%	+/-1.3%	0.7%	248
Victoria, TX	117,067	19,401	+/-3,355	16.6%	+/-2.9%	-3.6%	167
Vineland-Millville-Bridgeton, NJ	144,656	27,197	+/-3,841	18.8%	+/-2.6%	2.7%	100
Virginia Beach-Norfolk-Newport News, VA-NC	1,626,361	212,979	+/-9,984	13.1%	+/-0.6%	1.4% ▲	287
Visalia-Porterville, CA	444,186	135,194	+/-9,353	30.4%	+/-2.1%	4.7% ▲	4
Waco, TX	229,172	45,165	+/-5,494	19.7%	+/-2.4%	-4.7% ▼	88
Warner Robins, GA	144,513	26,938	+/-4,533	18.6%	+/-3.1%	4.7% ▲	104
Washington-Arlington-Alexandria, DC-VA-MD-WV	5,702,639	477,661	+/-17,577	8.4%	+/-0.3%	0.1%	363
Waterloo-Cedar Falls, IA	160,359	18,654	+/-2,583	11.6%	+/-1.6%	-3.0% ▼	323
Wausau, WI	132,121	14,459	+/-2,968	10.9%	+/-2.2%	-0.2%	337
Wenatchee-East Wenatchee, WA	111,898	15,450	+/-3,367	13.8%	+/-3.0%	-2.6%	273
Wheeling, WV-OH	139,509	22,078	+/-2,682	15.8%	+/-1.9%	1.4%	203
Wichita Falls, TX	136,506	19,432	+/-2,908	14.2%	+/-2.1%	0.4%	264
Wichita, KS	617,291	93,248	+/-7,402	15.1%	+/-1.2%	0.3%	229
Williamsport, PA	111,533	14,419	+/-2,792	12.9%	+/-2.5%	-1.0%	292
Wilmington, NC	368,099	60,100	+/-6,701	16.3%	+/-1.8%	-2.0%	182
Winchester, VA-WV	127,564	15,102	+/-2,939	11.8%	+/-2.3%	-2.7%	318
Winston-Salem, NC	473,311	99,551	+/-7,275	21.0%	+/-1.5%	2.9% ▲	55
Worcester, MA	781,577	92,497	+/-7,889	11.8%	+/-1.0%	0.2%	319
Yakima, WA	242,336	55,924	+/-5,630	23.1%	+/-2.3%	0.1%	29
York-Hanover, PA	429,553	45,934	+/-5,477	10.7%	+/-1.3%	-0.4%	340
Youngstown-Warren-Boardman, OH-PA	538,148	93,322	+/-5,882	17.3%	+/-1.1%	1.2%	147

		Number Poor		Poverty Rate (Percent Poor)			
Metropolitan Area	Total Population	Estimate	Margin of Error[a]	Poverty Rate	Margin of Error[a]	Difference 2011 vs. 2010 Poverty Rate[b]	Rank[c]
Yuba City, CA	165,603	36,260	+/-4,743	21.9%	+/-2.9%	5.6% ▲	43
Yuma, AZ	191,534	41,313	+/-5,377	21.6%	+/-2.8%	-0.3%	48
Number of metropolitan areas with a statistically significant change in poverty from 2011 to 2012:					Increase	▲ 26	
					Decrease	▼ 25	

Source: Table prepared by the Congressional Research Service (CRS) based on analysis of U.S. Census Bureau 2012 and 2011 American Community Survey (ACS) data, table series S1701: Poverty Status in the Past 12 Months, from the Census Bureau's American FactFinder, available on the Internet at http://factfinder2.census.gov/faces/nav/jsf/pages/index.xhtml.

a. Margin of error of an estimate based on a 90% statistical confidence level. When added to and subtracted from an estimate, the range reflects a 90% statistical confidence interval bounding the estimate.

b. Statistically significant increase in poverty at the 90% statistical confidence level: ▲. Statistically significant decrease in poverty at the 90% statistical confidence level: ▼.

c. Ranks are based on areas' poverty rate estimates for 2011. Because of sampling variability, an area's rank does not statistically differ from other areas with overlapping margins of error.

Appendix C. Poverty Estimates by Congressional District

Table C-1. Poverty by Congressional District: 2012

		Number Poor		Poverty Rate (Percent Poor)		
Congressional District	Total Population	Estimate	Margin of Error[a]	Estimate	Margin of Error[a]	Rank[b]
Alabama						
1st	676,609	130,649	+/-8,345	19.3%	1.2%	104
2nd	663,476	127,765	+/-7,179	19.3%	1.1%	104
3rd	675,905	148,090	+/-9,664	21.9%	1.4%	67
4th	672,170	128,918	+/-9,118	19.2%	1.4%	108
5th	682,028	96,033	+/-8,233	14.1%	1.2%	254
6th	677,886	73,189	+/-7,066	10.8%	1.0%	357
7th	658,904	187,920	+/-10,141	28.5%	1.4%	17
Alaska						
(at Large)	715,608	72,400	+/-5,190	10.1%	0.7%	374
Arizona						
1st	695,794	152,487	+/-8,214	21.9%	1.1%	67
2nd	705,345	117,221	+/-8,290	16.6%	1.1%	174
3rd	693,235	174,597	+/-13,094	25.2%	1.7%	36
4th	689,367	113,908	+/-11,515	16.5%	1.6%	178
5th	733,015	71,479	+/-7,721	9.8%	1.0%	378
6th	718,323	94,570	+/-10,433	13.2%	1.3%	281
7th	725,159	263,298	+/-12,104	36.3%	1.6%	3
8th	718,476	67,993	+/-6,728	9.5%	0.9%	385
9th	722,559	138,953	+/-11,779	19.2%	1.6%	108
Arkansas						
1st	700,063	154,691	+/-8,708	22.1%	1.3%	60
2nd	731,940	121,956	+/-9,669	16.7%	1.3%	171
3rd	736,689	137,947	+/-8,851	18.7%	1.2%	121
4th	696,406	153,471	+/-8,346	22.0%	1.2%	64

Congressional District	Total Population	Number Poor		Poverty Rate (Percent Poor)		
		Estimate	Margin of Error[a]	Estimate	Margin of Error[a]	Rank[b]
California						
1st	689,144	127,862	+/-9,617	18.6%	1.4%	122
2nd	687,342	93,852	+/-6,481	13.7%	0.9%	266
3rd	689,519	122,750	+/-9,503	17.8%	1.4%	149
4th	692,082	74,698	+/-8,377	10.8%	1.2%	357
5th	704,362	91,086	+/-7,690	12.9%	1.1%	291
6th	706,841	168,979	+/-10,560	23.9%	1.4%	46
7th	708,853	108,182	+/-9,523	15.3%	1.3%	209
8th	690,267	166,240	+/-13,322	24.1%	1.9%	44
9th	713,639	130,861	+/-10,608	18.3%	1.5%	132
10th	703,775	124,240	+/-11,074	17.7%	1.6%	152
11th	718,213	91,058	+/-9,735	12.7%	1.3%	299
12th	705,993	105,694	+/-8,440	15.0%	1.1%	222
13th	700,707	123,485	+/-8,330	17.6%	1.2%	156
14th	718,542	69,511	+/-7,500	9.7%	1.0%	380
15th	722,379	65,209	+/-6,212	9.0%	0.9%	392
16th	696,824	219,915	+/-11,765	31.6%	1.5%	7
17th	711,893	61,582	+/-8,456	8.7%	1.2%	397
18th	723,289	53,567	+/-5,704	7.4%	0.8%	420
19th	704,736	100,484	+/-7,902	14.3%	1.1%	242
20th	691,893	117,282	+/-10,227	17.0%	1.5%	167
21st	668,049	209,012	+/-11,618	31.3%	1.6%	8
22nd	707,203	166,252	+/-13,593	23.5%	1.7%	50
23rd	692,520	132,054	+/-12,510	19.1%	1.7%	112
24th	682,216	105,159	+/-7,306	15.4%	1.1%	205
25th	705,022	114,612	+/-9,605	16.3%	1.3%	180
26th	701,681	82,431	+/-7,749	11.7%	1.1%	334
27th	699,048	86,217	+/-8,030	12.3%	1.1%	316
28th	722,438	117,701	+/-8,333	16.3%	1.1%	180
29th	714,921	169,736	+/-11,962	23.7%	1.5%	48
30th	720,239	91,833	+/-9,277	12.8%	1.2%	296
31st	708,296	144,480	+/-10,618	20.4%	1.5%	82
32nd	707,524	105,916	+/-9,182	15.0%	1.3%	222
33rd	681,740	60,822	+/-5,962	8.9%	0.9%	394
34th	692,893	206,176	+/-12,226	29.8%	1.6%	9

Congressional District	Total Population	Number Poor: Estimate	Number Poor: Margin of Error[a]	Poverty Rate (Percent Poor): Estimate	Poverty Rate (Percent Poor): Margin of Error[a]	Rank[b]
35th	700,898	127,234	+/-12,498	18.2%	1.7%	136
36th	701,988	154,852	+/-10,948	22.1%	1.5%	60
37th	703,123	164,669	+/-12,158	23.4%	1.5%	52
38th	707,001	95,743	+/-7,409	13.5%	1.0%	273
39th	711,830	74,272	+/-7,800	10.4%	1.1%	365
40th	689,588	201,746	+/-12,781	29.3%	1.6%	12
41st	713,695	156,762	+/-11,029	22.0%	1.5%	64
42nd	737,152	81,528	+/-9,973	11.1%	1.4%	351
43rd	688,928	140,891	+/-8,409	20.5%	1.1%	81
44th	706,530	177,254	+/-11,313	25.1%	1.5%	37
45th	715,291	60,097	+/-6,778	8.4%	0.9%	399
46th	702,019	139,347	+/-9,883	19.8%	1.4%	96
47th	715,431	139,437	+/-10,340	19.5%	1.4%	100
48th	712,933	76,416	+/-7,636	10.7%	1.0%	360
49th	692,263	81,897	+/-8,077	11.8%	1.2%	331
50th	716,105	112,661	+/-11,544	15.7%	1.6%	196
51st	704,825	174,803	+/-11,350	24.8%	1.5%	40
52nd	683,708	60,789	+/-7,010	8.9%	1.0%	394
53rd	715,875	95,983	+/-8,718	13.4%	1.2%	278
Colorado						
1st	737,921	131,952	+/-8,254	17.9%	1.1%	143
2nd	725,067	89,148	+/-6,172	12.3%	0.8%	316
3rd	703,743	117,691	+/-9,306	16.7%	1.3%	171
4th	719,106	89,425	+/-8,256	12.4%	1.1%	313
5th	710,194	92,466	+/-8,949	13.0%	1.3%	289
6th	740,881	82,638	+/-7,116	11.2%	1.0%	348
7th	732,159	91,522	+/-8,698	12.5%	1.2%	309
Connecticut						
1st	708,207	87,135	+/-6,856	12.3%	1.0%	316
2nd	671,223	53,776	+/-5,017	8.0%	0.7%	406
3rd	688,707	83,544	+/-6,949	12.1%	1.0%	322
4th	715,943	68,567	+/-6,765	9.6%	0.9%	383
5th	700,098	79,368	+/-6,415	11.3%	0.9%	344

Congressional District	Total Population	Number Poor: Estimate	Number Poor: Margin of Error[a]	Poverty Rate (Percent Poor): Estimate	Poverty Rate (Percent Poor): Margin of Error[a]	Rank[b]
Delaware						
(at Large)	890,738	107,307	+/-7,877	12.0%	0.9%	327
District of Columbia						
Delegate District (at Large)	598,151	108,732	+/-7,746	18.2%	1.3%	136
Florida						
1st	688,243	105,427	+/-8,363	15.3%	1.2%	209
2nd	659,760	132,329	+/-9,610	20.1%	1.4%	90
3rd	664,128	135,279	+/-11,765	20.4%	1.7%	82
4th	688,250	88,268	+/-9,166	12.8%	1.3%	296
5th	696,603	196,707	+/-14,655	28.2%	1.7%	20
6th	697,635	120,509	+/-8,745	17.3%	1.2%	162
7th	699,230	101,104	+/-10,415	14.5%	1.4%	236
8th	694,193	105,439	+/-9,283	15.2%	1.3%	215
9th	727,426	138,152	+/-13,332	19.0%	1.7%	115
10th	712,761	103,003	+/-10,923	14.5%	1.5%	236
11th	682,125	120,282	+/-9,177	17.6%	1.3%	156
12th	686,651	78,423	+/-7,348	11.4%	1.0%	341
13th	691,141	91,076	+/-8,021	13.2%	1.1%	281
14th	726,663	180,189	+/-13,337	24.8%	1.7%	40
15th	689,811	108,281	+/-8,995	15.7%	1.2%	196
16th	704,435	96,755	+/-8,384	13.7%	1.2%	266
17th	688,530	123,506	+/-11,269	17.9%	1.5%	143
18th	703,827	97,577	+/-10,639	13.9%	1.5%	257
19th	711,333	98,726	+/-7,543	13.9%	1.0%	257
20th	714,377	165,867	+/-13,255	23.2%	1.7%	53
21st	714,851	79,327	+/-7,769	11.1%	1.1%	351
22nd	692,931	99,591	+/-8,695	14.4%	1.2%	239
23rd	724,621	102,593	+/-9,784	14.2%	1.4%	247
24th	712,946	182,532	+/-13,479	25.6%	1.7%	34
25th	707,017	117,394	+/-9,432	16.6%	1.3%	174
26th	715,896	116,829	+/-10,908	16.3%	1.4%	180

Congressional District	Total Population	Number Poor: Estimate	Number Poor: Margin of Error[a]	Poverty Rate (Percent Poor): Estimate	Poverty Rate (Percent Poor): Margin of Error[a]	Rank[b]
27th	717,095	153,416	+/-11,348	21.4%	1.5%	72
Georgia						
1st	690,455	126,391	+/-8,479	18.3%	1.2%	132
2nd	653,169	185,101	+/-8,304	28.3%	1.3%	18
3rd	691,331	113,054	+/-10,064	16.4%	1.4%	179
4th	707,173	141,794	+/-13,685	20.1%	1.8%	90
5th	693,605	182,143	+/-11,442	26.3%	1.6%	31
6th	714,317	74,617	+/-9,072	10.4%	1.2%	365
7th	710,922	92,032	+/-11,076	12.9%	1.5%	291
8th	677,554	147,963	+/-10,029	21.8%	1.5%	69
9th	691,318	128,041	+/-9,544	18.5%	1.4%	127
10th	683,685	128,934	+/-8,906	18.9%	1.3%	117
11th	694,853	87,315	+/-10,902	12.6%	1.5%	303
12th	666,610	165,669	+/-9,704	24.9%	1.4%	38
13th	699,598	145,643	+/-12,268	20.8%	1.6%	79
14th	678,006	129,836	+/-10,081	19.1%	1.5%	112
Hawaii						
1st	674,348	67,252	+/-6,798	10.0%	1.0%	376
2nd	682,474	89,991	+/-7,548	13.2%	1.1%	281
Idaho						
1st	783,009	123,748	+/-9,660	15.8%	1.2%	194
2nd	782,502	124,746	+/-9,762	15.9%	1.2%	192
Illinois						
1st	697,333	143,852	+/-11,064	20.6%	1.4%	80
2nd	700,318	158,034	+/-10,050	22.6%	1.4%	58
3rd	694,448	83,155	+/-9,528	12.0%	1.3%	327
4th	708,675	154,012	+/-10,643	21.7%	1.4%	70
5th	708,786	80,640	+/-8,030	11.4%	1.0%	341
6th	716,448	41,945	+/-5,809	5.9%	0.8%	430
7th	715,934	196,478	+/-11,969	27.4%	1.5%	26
8th	720,719	71,925	+/-7,187	10.0%	1.0%	376

Congressional District	Total Population	Number Poor		Poverty Rate (Percent Poor)		
		Estimate	Margin of Error[a]	Estimate	Margin of Error[a]	Rank[b]
9th	700,161	94,600	+/-9,628	13.5%	1.3%	273
10th	689,660	71,662	+/-7,492	10.4%	1.1%	365
11th	714,183	78,426	+/-8,211	11.0%	1.2%	354
12th	687,871	126,683	+/-7,174	18.4%	1.0%	129
13th	664,086	125,568	+/-7,760	18.9%	1.1%	117
14th	716,042	46,646	+/-6,793	6.5%	1.0%	426
15th	680,098	100,239	+/-7,047	14.7%	1.0%	227
16th	683,788	82,859	+/-6,380	12.1%	0.9%	322
17th	682,072	122,252	+/-5,953	17.9%	0.8%	143
18th	693,054	71,586	+/-5,802	10.3%	0.8%	369
Indiana						
1st	703,029	124,823	+/-9,093	17.8%	1.3%	149
2nd	695,790	105,380	+/-8,404	15.1%	1.2%	218
3rd	711,671	104,830	+/-7,842	14.7%	1.1%	227
4th	702,183	93,809	+/-6,442	13.4%	0.9%	278
5th	716,607	64,543	+/-6,415	9.0%	0.9%	392
6th	697,681	110,078	+/-7,147	15.8%	1.0%	194
7th	720,385	175,849	+/-11,361	24.4%	1.5%	43
8th	690,935	101,500	+/-7,483	14.7%	1.1%	227
9th	704,142	109,513	+/-6,835	15.6%	0.9%	200
Iowa						
1st	738,176	81,782	+/-5,188	11.1%	0.7%	351
2nd	743,195	105,364	+/-6,182	14.2%	0.8%	247
3rd	762,670	91,998	+/-8,183	12.1%	1.1%	322
4th	730,184	98,340	+/-6,356	13.5%	0.9%	273
Kansas						
1st	694,414	96,605	+/-6,681	13.9%	1.0%	257
2nd	682,707	113,104	+/-7,042	16.6%	1.0%	174
3rd	723,006	74,616	+/-6,452	10.3%	0.9%	369
4th	702,080	107,409	+/-7,777	15.3%	1.1%	209

Congressional District	Total Population	Number Poor: Estimate	Number Poor: Margin of Error[a]	Poverty Rate (Percent Poor): Estimate	Poverty Rate (Percent Poor): Margin of Error[a]	Rank[b]
Kentucky						
1st	699,397	140,495	+/-8,073	20.1%	1.1%	90
2nd	710,130	124,063	+/-8,418	17.5%	1.2%	159
3rd	719,003	132,171	+/-9,076	18.4%	1.3%	129
4th	717,267	105,068	+/-8,029	14.6%	1.1%	232
5th	692,823	190,713	+/-10,303	27.5%	1.5%	24
6th	708,483	130,687	+/-8,915	18.4%	1.2%	129
Louisiana						
1st	699,397	140,495	+/-8,073	20.1%	1.1%	90
2nd	710,130	124,063	+/-8,418	17.5%	1.2%	159
3rd	719,003	132,171	+/-9,076	18.4%	1.3%	129
4th	717,267	105,068	+/-8,029	14.6%	1.1%	232
5th	692,823	190,713	+/-10,303	27.5%	1.5%	24
6th	708,483	130,687	+/-8,915	18.4%	1.2%	129
Maine						
1st	650,449	81,891	+/-7,036	12.6%	1.1%	303
2nd	643,008	107,895	+/-7,136	16.8%	1.1%	169
Maryland						
1st	708,143	73,635	+/-6,877	10.4%	1.0%	365
2nd	713,531	90,176	+/-8,593	12.6%	1.1%	303
3rd	705,600	57,045	+/-6,684	8.1%	0.9%	403
4th	725,479	69,932	+/-6,740	9.6%	0.9%	383
5th	716,527	54,966	+/-6,877	7.7%	0.9%	415
6th	722,666	67,629	+/-6,074	9.4%	0.9%	389
7th	715,061	127,932	+/-8,982	17.9%	1.2%	143
8th	737,438	49,488	+/-5,889	6.7%	0.8%	424
Massachusetts						
1st	700,591	113,390	+/-7,681	16.2%	1.1%	186
2nd	707,029	90,167	+/-7,901	12.8%	1.1%	296
3rd	716,733	91,302	+/-9,025	12.7%	1.3%	299
4th	707,925	55,732	+/-5,792	7.9%	0.8%	411

Congressional District	Total Population	Number Poor: Estimate	Number Poor: Margin of Error[a]	Poverty Rate (Percent Poor): Estimate	Poverty Rate (Percent Poor): Margin of Error[a]	Rank[b]
5th	716,981	60,448	+/-6,237	8.4%	0.9%	399
6th	728,714	58,295	+/-5,684	8.0%	0.8%	406
7th	694,284	147,787	+/-9,695	21.3%	1.4%	75
8th	727,811	70,537	+/-7,353	9.7%	1.0%	380
9th	714,694	74,987	+/-5,983	10.5%	0.8%	362
Michigan						
1st	677,503	104,488	+/-5,801	15.4%	0.8%	205
2nd	690,343	112,751	+/-7,428	16.3%	1.1%	180
3rd	698,624	117,769	+/-8,371	16.9%	1.2%	168
4th	674,517	117,246	+/-7,484	17.4%	1.1%	161
5th	687,424	140,231	+/-8,179	20.4%	1.2%	82
6th	693,214	122,724	+/-7,517	17.7%	1.1%	152
7th	679,746	91,436	+/-6,174	13.5%	0.9%	273
8th	686,960	94,508	+/-6,454	13.8%	0.9%	262
9th	706,069	96,451	+/-7,642	13.7%	1.1%	266
10th	694,228	77,810	+/-5,212	11.2%	0.7%	348
11th	710,800	55,848	+/-5,488	7.9%	0.8%	411
12th	689,178	130,962	+/-8,689	19.0%	1.2%	115
13th	688,257	230,880	+/-11,840	33.5%	1.6%	4
14th	686,897	192,074	+/-11,943	28.0%	1.6%	21
Minnesota						
1st	643,739	75,074	+/-5,409	11.7%	0.8%	334
2nd	662,264	47,739	+/-4,935	7.2%	0.7%	422
3rd	673,470	45,966	+/-5,109	6.8%	0.8%	423
4th	661,977	93,466	+/-5,999	14.1%	0.9%	254
5th	665,875	123,217	+/-7,583	18.5%	1.1%	127
6th	662,919	52,480	+/-4,768	7.9%	0.7%	411
7th	642,977	75,097	+/-3,737	11.7%	0.6%	334
8th	644,222	85,332	+/-4,498	13.2%	0.7%	281
Mississippi						
1st	731,105	147,955	+/-9,226	20.2%	1.2%	86
2nd	698,141	226,545	+/-10,816	32.4%	1.5%	6

Congressional District	Total Population	Number Poor Estimate	Number Poor Margin of Error[a]	Poverty Rate (Percent Poor) Estimate	Poverty Rate (Percent Poor) Margin of Error[a]	Rank[b]
3rd	725,942	160,309	+/-10,556	22.1%	1.4%	60
4th	735,702	163,443	+/-11,011	22.2%	1.5%	59
Missouri						
1st	718,265	172,959	+/-10,029	24.1%	1.4%	44
2nd	747,083	48,691	+/-5,977	6.5%	0.8%	426
3rd	735,959	95,467	+/-9,436	13.0%	1.3%	289
4th	716,487	123,770	+/-7,136	17.3%	1.0%	162
5th	738,266	143,544	+/-8,889	19.4%	1.2%	103
6th	725,542	84,418	+/-6,881	11.6%	0.9%	338
7th	734,955	136,899	+/-8,262	18.6%	1.1%	122
8th	721,451	142,044	+/-7,419	19.7%	1.0%	98
Montana						
(at Large)	980,594	152,199	+/-8,004	15.5%	0.8%	201
Nebraska						
1st	599,561	75,024	+/-6,296	12.5%	1.0%	309
2nd	613,521	85,350	+/-6,395	13.9%	1.0%	257
3rd	587,822	73,599	+/-4,596	12.5%	0.8%	309
Nevada						
1st	663,180	156,130	+/-11,181	23.5%	1.6%	50
2nd	675,424	113,211	+/-8,921	16.8%	1.3%	169
3rd	706,700	62,437	+/-8,791	8.8%	1.2%	396
4th	673,261	115,062	+/-9,991	17.1%	1.5%	165
New Hampshire						
1st	641,872	67,610	+/-7,372	10.5%	1.2%	362
2nd	638,155	60,856	+/-7,179	9.5%	1.1%	385
New Jersey						
1st	719,015	86,078	+/-7,870	12.0%	1.1%	327
2nd	710,671	90,165	+/-8,117	12.7%	1.1%	299
3rd	727,214	48,527	+/-5,466	6.7%	0.8%	424

Congressional District	Total Population	Number Poor		Poverty Rate (Percent Poor)		
		Estimate	Margin of Error[a]	Estimate	Margin of Error[a]	Rank[b]
4th	723,605	68,879	+/-7,577	9.5%	1.0%	385
5th	729,002	42,698	+/-6,006	5.9%	0.8%	430
6th	714,808	77,573	+/-6,980	10.9%	1.0%	355
7th	735,414	36,228	+/-5,120	4.9%	0.7%	436
8th	750,467	132,305	+/-9,479	17.6%	1.3%	156
9th	741,848	111,406	+/-9,336	15.0%	1.3%	222
10th	701,721	141,521	+/-8,682	20.2%	1.2%	86
11th	715,572	31,021	+/-4,588	4.3%	0.6%	437
12th	722,336	68,542	+/-8,105	9.5%	1.1%	385
New Mexico						
1st	682,060	130,830	+/-9,858	19.2%	1.4%	108
2nd	679,970	157,479	+/-9,774	23.2%	1.4%	53
3rd	682,748	137,936	+/-6,781	20.2%	1.0%	86
New York						
1st	701,977	52,081	+/-8,134	7.4%	1.2%	420
2nd	715,982	43,357	+/-6,355	6.1%	0.9%	429
3rd	703,367	40,731	+/-6,534	5.8%	0.9%	432
4th	711,464	54,786	+/-7,419	7.7%	1.0%	415
5th	744,436	113,951	+/-9,669	15.3%	1.2%	209
6th	718,016	108,636	+/-10,658	15.1%	1.4%	218
7th	743,170	219,015	+/-12,229	29.5%	1.4%	10
8th	716,323	175,873	+/-10,595	24.6%	1.3%	42
9th	726,691	144,479	+/-11,685	19.9%	1.5%	95
10th	705,022	117,770	+/-9,334	16.7%	1.2%	171
11th	723,626	99,680	+/-8,737	13.8%	1.2%	262
12th	683,519	82,653	+/-8,773	12.1%	1.2%	322
13th	747,166	211,491	+/-14,013	28.3%	1.7%	18
14th	708,425	132,848	+/-11,483	18.8%	1.5%	119
15th	714,454	293,196	+/-12,261	41.0%	1.6%	2
16th	713,039	102,064	+/-7,936	14.3%	1.1%	242
17th	713,627	82,291	+/-7,445	11.5%	1.1%	340
18th	692,091	71,329	+/-6,300	10.3%	0.9%	369
19th	680,646	85,899	+/-5,298	12.6%	0.8%	303

Congressional District	Total Population	Number Poor: Estimate	Number Poor: Margin of Error[a]	Poverty Rate (Percent Poor): Estimate	Poverty Rate: Margin of Error[a]	Rank[b]
20th	694,840	85,219	+/-5,791	12.3%	0.8%	316
21st	678,292	93,116	+/-7,026	13.7%	1.0%	266
22nd	682,661	105,839	+/-6,654	15.5%	0.9%	201
23rd	675,791	112,369	+/-5,895	16.6%	0.9%	174
24th	684,084	99,676	+/-6,531	14.6%	0.9%	232
25th	698,243	107,280	+/-6,423	15.4%	0.9%	205
26th	693,890	129,249	+/-7,462	18.6%	1.1%	122
27th	693,222	60,138	+/-5,789	8.7%	0.8%	397
North Carolina						
1st	702,539	201,661	+/-11,692	28.7%	1.6%	13
2nd	751,063	113,158	+/-7,650	15.1%	1.0%	218
3rd	713,733	115,326	+/-9,206	16.2%	1.2%	186
4th	724,081	132,558	+/-10,840	18.3%	1.4%	132
5th	721,961	138,292	+/-10,576	19.2%	1.4%	108
6th	723,116	102,710	+/-9,247	14.2%	1.2%	247
7th	738,207	133,212	+/-11,407	18.0%	1.5%	142
8th	723,921	152,569	+/-8,559	21.1%	1.2%	77
9th	755,552	60,758	+/-7,311	8.0%	0.9%	406
10th	727,845	131,579	+/-9,026	18.1%	1.2%	140
11th	716,698	133,351	+/-7,947	18.6%	1.1%	122
12th	749,706	206,306	+/-13,029	27.5%	1.6%	24
13th	750,571	91,652	+/-9,414	12.2%	1.2%	321
North Dakota						
(at Large)	674,852	75,703	+/-4,270	11.2%	0.6%	348
Ohio						
1st	711,840	129,122	+/-7,753	18.1%	1.0%	140
2nd	701,728	110,085	+/-8,490	15.7%	1.1%	196
3rd	712,972	169,589	+/-10,869	23.8%	1.5%	47
4th	687,594	99,274	+/-7,180	14.4%	1.1%	239
5th	707,281	97,188	+/-6,938	13.7%	1.0%	266
6th	693,005	112,371	+/-8,050	16.2%	1.1%	186
7th	709,830	93,903	+/-7,178	13.2%	1.0%	281

Congressional District	Total Population	Number Poor		Poverty Rate (Percent Poor)		
		Estimate	Margin of Error[a]	Estimate	Margin of Error[a]	Rank[b]
8th	707,376	105,171	+/-7,360	14.9%	1.0%	226
9th	693,929	158,035	+/-8,423	22.8%	1.1%	56
10th	695,215	122,787	+/-9,295	17.7%	1.3%	152
11th	678,366	186,993	+/-9,329	27.6%	1.3%	22
12th	719,437	81,492	+/-7,181	11.3%	1.0%	344
13th	693,471	135,004	+/-7,562	19.5%	1.1%	100
14th	709,504	68,614	+/-6,341	9.7%	0.9%	380
15th	694,971	101,994	+/-7,861	14.7%	1.1%	227
16th	710,963	53,006	+/-6,289	7.5%	0.9%	419
Oklahoma						
1st	752,052	115,981	+/-5,777	15.4%	0.8%	205
2nd	722,645	155,342	+/-6,301	21.5%	0.9%	71
3rd	726,375	106,677	+/-7,776	14.7%	1.1%	227
4th	743,691	106,418	+/-6,985	14.3%	0.9%	242
5th	754,890	153,011	+/-7,820	20.3%	1.0%	85
Oregon						
1st	777,086	107,498	+/-9,839	13.8%	1.3%	262
2nd	756,558	138,119	+/-9,067	18.3%	1.2%	132
3rd	775,068	135,606	+/-9,087	17.5%	1.2%	159
4th	754,174	160,941	+/-10,081	21.3%	1.3%	75
5th	763,512	116,195	+/-9,357	15.2%	1.2%	215
Pennsylvania						
1st	694,928	177,972	+/-13,028	25.6%	1.7%	34
2nd	682,233	195,552	+/-11,307	28.7%	1.5%	13
3rd	675,649	93,557	+/-5,085	13.8%	0.7%	262
4th	692,259	81,450	+/-7,526	11.8%	1.1%	331
5th	657,341	103,067	+/-6,055	15.7%	0.9%	196
6th	702,574	56,813	+/-6,214	8.1%	0.9%	403
7th	693,713	44,474	+/-5,342	6.4%	0.8%	428
8th	701,486	37,390	+/-4,455	5.3%	0.6%	435
9th	684,936	103,275	+/-5,772	15.1%	0.8%	218
10th	678,535	96,163	+/-7,476	14.2%	1.1%	247

Congressional District	Total Population	Number Poor: Estimate	Number Poor: Margin of Error[a]	Poverty Rate (Percent Poor): Estimate	Poverty Rate (Percent Poor): Margin of Error[a]	Rank[b]
11th	673,464	83,737	+/-6,083	12.4%	0.9%	313
12th	686,656	64,703	+/-5,394	9.4%	0.8%	389
13th	705,851	100,456	+/-10,048	14.2%	1.3%	247
14th	684,186	124,287	+/-7,409	18.2%	1.1%	136
15th	686,301	78,406	+/-6,510	11.4%	1.0%	341
16th	687,523	104,692	+/-8,487	15.2%	1.2%	215
17th	682,298	92,723	+/-7,351	13.6%	1.1%	271
18th	683,934	54,568	+/-5,729	8.0%	0.8%	406
Puerto Rico						
Resident Commissioner District (at Large)	3,633,892	1,632,533	+/-27,010	44.9%	0.7%	1
Rhode Island						
1st	513,714	82,717	+/-6,573	16.1%	1.3%	189
2nd	496,735	56,190	+/-5,442	11.3%	1.1%	344
South Carolina						
1st	688,883	81,973	+/-8,007	11.9%	1.1%	330
2nd	653,014	93,046	+/-9,135	14.2%	1.4%	247
3rd	642,671	124,218	+/-9,203	19.3%	1.4%	104
4th	656,127	117,464	+/-9,012	17.9%	1.3%	143
5th	661,102	118,057	+/-9,506	17.9%	1.4%	143
6th	624,208	161,887	+/-7,913	25.9%	1.2%	33
7th	659,449	141,125	+/-9,162	21.4%	1.4%	72
South Dakota						
(at Large)	804,310	107,846	+/-5,355	13.4%	0.7%	278
Tennessee						
1st	694,785	135,472	+/-9,287	19.5%	1.3%	100
2nd	695,352	113,657	+/-7,644	16.3%	1.1%	180
3rd	693,756	119,764	+/-7,751	17.3%	1.1%	162
4th	704,373	120,450	+/-7,496	17.1%	1.1%	165
5th	701,692	131,716	+/-9,197	18.8%	1.3%	119

Congressional District	Total Population	Number Poor Estimate	Number Poor Margin of Error[a]	Poverty Rate (Percent Poor) Estimate	Poverty Rate Margin of Error[a]	Rank[b]
6th	712,354	106,622	+/-7,449	15.0%	1.0%	222
7th	705,399	115,116	+/-8,767	16.3%	1.2%	180
8th	686,751	95,688	+/-7,299	13.9%	1.1%	257
9th	701,532	190,845	+/-10,199	27.2%	1.5%	27
Texas						
1st	686,626	132,633	+/-8,731	19.3%	1.3%	104
2nd	735,559	80,473	+/-10,464	10.9%	1.3%	355
3rd	743,221	58,944	+/-9,199	7.9%	1.2%	411
4th	685,420	121,083	+/-6,702	17.7%	1.0%	152
5th	686,893	151,407	+/-10,355	22.0%	1.5%	64
6th	713,424	87,809	+/-9,286	12.3%	1.3%	316
7th	716,136	76,927	+/-10,122	10.7%	1.3%	360
8th	705,717	100,759	+/-12,304	14.3%	1.7%	242
9th	735,236	174,569	+/-13,397	23.7%	1.8%	48
10th	692,729	91,446	+/-9,570	13.2%	1.3%	281
11th	694,987	97,153	+/-6,618	14.0%	1.0%	256
12th	712,788	92,145	+/-9,332	12.9%	1.2%	291
13th	669,921	107,798	+/-8,461	16.1%	1.2%	189
14th	672,407	102,657	+/-7,909	15.3%	1.2%	209
15th	703,090	201,440	+/-14,333	28.7%	1.9%	13
16th	708,994	156,524	+/-10,480	22.1%	1.5%	60
17th	685,958	137,611	+/-9,994	20.1%	1.4%	90
18th	712,473	192,572	+/-13,952	27.0%	1.7%	29
19th	669,161	131,061	+/-8,040	19.6%	1.2%	99
20th	707,547	151,767	+/-11,496	21.4%	1.5%	72
21st	716,699	94,145	+/-8,141	13.1%	1.1%	288
22nd	744,596	62,307	+/-9,572	8.4%	1.2%	399
23rd	695,340	146,751	+/-11,677	21.1%	1.5%	77
24th	729,154	82,467	+/-10,331	11.3%	1.3%	344
25th	699,066	102,216	+/-9,642	14.6%	1.3%	232
26th	736,511	59,062	+/-8,131	8.0%	1.1%	406
27th	697,373	110,691	+/-7,763	15.9%	1.1%	192
28th	722,981	199,542	+/-12,876	27.6%	1.7%	22
29th	692,970	199,225	+/-16,001	28.7%	1.9%	13

		Number Poor		Poverty Rate (Percent Poor)		
Congressional District	Total Population	Estimate	Margin of Error[a]	Estimate	Margin of Error[a]	Rank[b]
30th	710,670	163,565	+/-10,680	23.0%	1.4%	55
31st	724,994	75,033	+/-6,475	10.3%	0.9%	369
32nd	728,358	95,892	+/-10,577	13.2%	1.4%	281
33rd	696,998	205,237	+/-12,199	29.4%	1.5%	11
34th	695,220	226,937	+/-15,470	32.6%	2.2%	5
35th	728,310	191,327	+/-15,862	26.3%	1.9%	31
36th	692,991	101,177	+/-9,430	14.6%	1.3%	232
Utah						
1st	700,960	81,475	+/-8,448	11.6%	1.2%	338
2nd	689,516	98,982	+/-8,903	14.4%	1.3%	239
3rd	697,053	89,983	+/-8,387	12.9%	1.2%	291
4th	718,491	89,577	+/-9,334	12.5%	1.3%	309
Vermont						
(at Large)	601,611	71,084	+/-4,549	11.8%	0.8%	331
Virginia						
1st	726,362	58,886	+/-6,992	8.1%	0.9%	403
2nd	691,193	74,617	+/-6,667	10.8%	0.9%	357
3rd	720,367	163,174	+/-11,407	22.7%	1.5%	57
4th	707,354	74,418	+/-6,928	10.5%	1.0%	362
5th	694,475	111,993	+/-8,143	16.1%	1.2%	189
6th	704,295	109,294	+/-8,174	15.5%	1.2%	201
7th	725,755	55,075	+/-6,263	7.6%	0.9%	418
8th	760,783	58,944	+/-6,710	7.7%	0.9%	415
9th	691,893	138,566	+/-7,286	20.0%	1.1%	94
10th	751,811	42,448	+/-5,677	5.6%	0.7%	434
11th	762,615	44,390	+/-6,062	5.8%	0.8%	432
Washington						
1st	684,375	62,325	+/-5,678	9.1%	0.8%	391
2nd	676,276	85,290	+/-7,859	12.6%	1.1%	303
3rd	678,767	92,153	+/-8,157	13.6%	1.2%	271
4th	683,388	127,216	+/-9,095	18.6%	1.3%	122

Congressional District	Total Population	Number Poor: Estimate	Number Poor: Margin of Error[a]	Poverty Rate (Percent Poor): Estimate	Poverty Rate (Percent Poor): Margin of Error[a]	Rank[b]
5th	649,717	115,344	+/-8,437	17.8%	1.3%	149
6th	666,992	90,315	+/-5,771	13.5%	0.9%	273
7th	678,739	81,918	+/-7,414	12.1%	1.1%	322
8th	682,722	68,891	+/-7,143	10.1%	1.0%	374
9th	685,058	104,837	+/-9,663	15.3%	1.3%	209
10th	675,900	86,989	+/-9,044	12.9%	1.3%	291
West Virginia						
1st	589,496	112,314	+/-7,464	19.1%	1.3%	112
2nd	614,627	87,053	+/-7,001	14.2%	1.1%	247
3rd	597,008	120,688	+/-7,731	20.2%	1.3%	86
Wisconsin						
1st	698,439	81,787	+/-6,891	11.7%	1.0%	334
2nd	711,444	90,226	+/-6,152	12.7%	0.9%	299
3rd	679,199	97,089	+/-5,401	14.3%	0.8%	242
4th	698,342	185,095	+/-9,515	26.5%	1.4%	30
5th	702,524	57,786	+/-6,225	8.2%	0.9%	402
6th	682,445	66,944	+/-5,424	9.8%	0.8%	378
7th	696,531	86,069	+/-5,576	12.4%	0.8%	313
8th	704,210	72,360	+/-5,428	10.3%	0.8%	369
Wyoming						
(at Large)	561,445	71,019	+/-6,087	12.6%	1.1%	303

Source: Table prepared by the Congressional Research Service (CRS) based on analysis of U.S. Census Bureau 2012 American Community Survey (ACS) data, table series S1701: Poverty Status in the Past 12 Months, from the Census Bureau's American FactFinder, available on the Internet at http://factfinder2.census.gov/faces/nav/jsf/pages/index.xhtml.

a. Margin of error of an estimate based on a 90% statistical confidence level. When added to and subtracted from an estimate, the range reflects a 90% statistical confidence interval bounding the estimate.

b. Ranks are based on the Congressional Districts' poverty rate estimates for 2012. Because of sampling variability, a District's rank does not statistically differ from other areas with overlapping margins of error.

Author Contact Information

Thomas Gabe
Specialist in Social Policy
tgabe@crs.loc.gov, 7-7357

www.ingramcontent.com/pod-product-compliance
Lightning Source LLC
Chambersburg PA
CBHW080323290526
45790CB00005B/2155
* 9 7 8 1 5 0 3 2 7 7 2 3 6 *